Listening for God

VOLUME 1

Contemporary Literature and the Life of Faith

Listening for
GOD

VOLUME 1

lannery O'Connor • Frederick Buechner
Patricia Hampl • Raymond Carver
Annie Dillard • Alice Walker
Garrison Keillor • Richard Rodriguez

Paula J. Carlson & Peter S. Hawkins

Augsburg Fortress
MINNEAPOLIS

LISTENING FOR GOD, Volume 1
Contemporary Literature and the Life of Faith

This Reader is accompanied by a Leader Guide and a Videocassette.

Developed in cooperation with the Institute of Sacred Music, Worship and the Arts, Yale University, New Haven, Connecticut.

Production made possible in part by a grant from the Lilly Endowment, Inc., Indianapolis, Indiana.

Cover art: copyright © Artville (Getty)
Cover design: Chance•Nelson, Inc.
Editors: Scott Tunseth and Carolyn F. Lystig

Library of Congress Cataloging-in-Publication Data

Listening for God : contemporary literature and the life of faith /
    contributing editors, Paula J. Carlson, Peter S. Hawkins
        p.   cm.
    ISBN 0-8066-2715-8
    1. American literature—Christian authors.   2. Christian life—
Literary collections.   3. American literature—20th century.
4. Faith—Literary collections.   I. Carlson, Paula J.   II. Hawkins,
Peter S.
PS508.C54L57   1994
813'.54080382—dc20   93-50662
                                                                  CIP

The paper used in this publication meets the minimum requirements of American National Standard for Information Sciences—Permanence of Paper for Printed Library Materials, ANSI Z329.48-1984.

Manufactured in the U.S.A.   ISBN 0-8066-2715-8

Contents

Acknowledgments

"Revelation" from THE COMPLETE STORIES by Flannery O'Connor. Copyright ©
1971 by the Estate of Mary Flannery O'Connor. Reprinted by permission of Farrar,
Straus & Giroux, Inc. and Harold Matson Company

"The Dwarves in the Stable" from TELLING SECRETS by Frederick Buechner. Copyright
© 1991 by Frederick Buechnner. Reprinted by permission of HarperCollins Publishers Inc.

Excerpts from VIRGIN TIME by Patricia Hampl. Copyright © 1992 by Patricia Hampl.
Reprinted by permission of Farrar, Strauss & Giroux, Inc.

"A Small Good Thing" from WHERE I'M CALLING FROM by Raymond Carver.
Copyright © 1988 by Raymond Carver. Used with permission of Grove/Atlantic Monthly
Press.

"The Deer at Providencia" and "A Field of Silence" from TEACHING A STONE TO
TALK by Annie Dillard. Copyright © 1982 by Annie Dillard. Reprinted by permission
of HarperCollins Publishers, Inc.

"The Welcome Table" from IN LOVE AND TROUBLE: STORIES OF BLACK WOMEN,
copyright © 1970 Alice Walker, reprinted by permission of Harcourt Brace & Company.

"Exiles" and "Aprille" from LEAVING HOME by Garrison Keillor. Copyright © 1987 &
1989 by Garrison Keillor. Used by permission of Viking Penguin, a division of
Penguin Books USA Inc., Penguin Books Canada, and Faber & Faber Limited.

"Credo" from HUNGER OF MEMORY by Richard Rodriguez. Copyright © 1982 by
Richard Rodriguez. Reprinted by permission of David R. Godine, Publisher.

Introduction

Where do you listen for God? If truth be told, there are places more obvious than the assortment of contemporary stories and essays offered in this resource. To begin with, of course, there are the Scriptures: the historical narratives of the Old and New Testaments, the poetry of the psalms, the teaching of the epistles, even the "fiction" of the parables. But then there is also a whole body of literature that, while neither sacred nor scriptural, has nonetheless attained an authority within the community. Who would be surprised to hear someone say they had heard the word of God in Augustine's *Confessions*, or Dante's *Divine Comedy*, or Bunyan's *Pilgrim's Progress*, or even in C. S. Lewis's *Narnia Chronicles*? For in every case you would be dealing with literature explicit about its connections to the Christian tradition, more or less openly evangelical in its thrust, and unequivocal in its expression of the faith. You would be listening for the word of God in texts where generations before you had heard it spoken; you would be reading literature that has an undisputed place in church.

It is quite another matter, however, to step outside a familiar circle of reliable texts and wander freely in unexplored territory. Listening for God then entails the risky business of the unknown and uncertain. It means allowing yourself to listen to the sounds of your own culture in all its bewildering diversity but without knowing for sure what you'll find. It also means being willing to explore unlikely places, to read not only authors who are known to be Christian but to investigate the work of those whose religious commitments may be hard to pin down. It may even mean spending time with writers who used to be Christian but are no longer, or with others who, rather than leaving the fold, have never entered it in the first place.

In this collection, for instance, there are many different stances taken with regard to orthodox Christianity; the authors range from an ordained Presbyterian clergyman (Frederick Buechner), to practicing Christians (like Annie Dillard, Garrison Keillor, and Richard Rodriguez), to a "fellow traveler" (like Patricia Hampl), to someone who has moved away from Christian tradition to forge an eclectic religion of her own (Alice Walker). Given this variety, readers will find points of disagreement as well as of contact, reasons to be uncomfortable as well as to feel at home. The challenge will be to pay attention everywhere, no matter how unlikely the source and regardless of what an author's known faith position may be.

Not that all the writers included are forthcoming about their beliefs, for here too there is great diversity. At one end of the spectrum is Flannery O'Connor. Thanks to the essays and letters published after her death, we know the depth of her faith and the extent to which it informed her entire sense of vocation as a writer: "I see from the standpoint of Christian orthodoxy. This means that for me the meaning of life is centered in our Redemption by Christ and what I see in the world I see in its relation to that."[1] At the other extreme stands Raymond Carver, like O'Connor a master of the short story, but utterly unlike her in his reticence about God talk. When asked once if he was religious, Carver replied, "No, but I have to believe in miracles and the possibility of resurrection."[2] Indeed, like many people who have no formal connection to the church, Carver felt himself to have been "saved" not in traditional Christian terms but through his association with Alcoholics Anonymous. He was open in his reliance on the higher power to carry him out of his alcoholism and to steady him in the sobriety of his last eleven years of life.

Readers of this study resource will no doubt feel more comfortable with the inclusion of a Flannery O'Connor than of a Raymond Carver. After all, where else in contemporary American literature would one look for God if not in the work of someone praised as a leading Catholic writer, whose faith is amply attested to by what amounts to a brilliant body of Christian apologetics? Yet the inevitability of O'Connor's presence here would not always have been so foregone a conclusion.

Only thirty years ago the connection between her fiction and her faith was not at all clear. In her own lifetime, before her posthumous essays and letters in effect taught the public how to read her work in her way, there were few who understood her quite straightforward religious intentions: they, after all, had only her disconcerting fiction, her stories at once violent, grotesque, and hilarious. Secular reviewers of her first collection, *A Good Man Is Hard To Find*, found her stories "brutal and sarcastic," counting it a shame that "someone with so much talent should look upon life as a horror story."[3] Nor was she better appreciated by the bulk of her co-religionists. The pious took her to task for failing to give them the uplift they had a right to expect from Catholic fiction. So few of her readers, in other words, "got it."

The public finally caught up with O'Connor's self-assessment and recognized in the pages of her fiction the radically "God-conscious writer" she always insisted she was. But this discovery of an orthodox Christian behind the somewhat baffling prose is neither the expectation nor the desire of this collection as a whole. Instead, it represents an attempt to cast the net wider than the known household of faith, to include a writer like Raymond Carver, for instance, whose formal religious convictions seem to have been as spare as his prose style, and whose presence alongside such openly Christian writers as O'Connor and Buechner, Dillard and Rodriguez, may not at first make sense for a resource intended for use with church study groups. Some similar reservation might be felt over Patricia Hampl, who (unlike Carver) had an intensely religious upbringing, but who now feels herself more a seeker than a believer; someone who when pressed for a religious either/or will say, "God, yes, I believe in God" and then immediately afterward feel "false, ripped off."[4] Hampl searches for the contemplative life in ways that clearly differentiate her from Carver, whose focus appears limited to the secular world. Even so, her search is accompanied by major reservations about the Almighty. Rather than affirmation, she prefers her own version of the small good thing—silence. For her, the genuinely spiritual may lie precisely in what is left unsaid.

Neither Carver, Hampl, nor Walker are included in this resource because they are thought to become "more" Christian when placed in the company of others whose religious credentials are not in dispute. Rather, they are here because they offer their own witness to the spiritual life, because they demonstrate an authenticity that cannot be discounted, even if it fails to measure up to some standard of faith. Their very outsider status allows them to see otherwise, if not more, than those within the fold. In Carver's case there is the haunting beauty of stories like "A Small Good Thing," with their evocation of something far more rich and profound than the bare human condition they apparently narrate. With Hampl, on the other hand, there is the poignancy of a pilgrim spirit who cannot quite find her pilgrimage, the dilemma of an uneasy seeker no longer able to define her search but keeping it going nonetheless. If Carver's work does not in any obvious way "belong" in church, Hampl's does so only tentatively, with a door propped open for hasty retreat. Yet both portray human life as a mystery for which contemporary secularity simply does not render a sufficient account. They show us miracles of grace erupting outside the context of formal religion (where grace, as the Scriptures show us, has always most abounded). They invite the reader to explore the spiritual territory their writing opens up but in no way "settles"; they prompt us to ask religious questions that they themselves do not answer.

Jesus himself, of course, was a master of parable, a storyteller whose "fictions" ask infinitely more than they ever answer. They are also striking in their refusal to wear religion on their sleeve, indeed striking in their avoidance of conventional spirituality. These aspects of Jesus' "art" may, in fact, have caused the early church some concern. His open narrative style, his penchant for not making the point explicitly, seem to have made the evangelists nervous about all that was *not* being said. For given his spare, unadorned stories about unjust judges and crafty servants, about one man who discovers buried treasure and another who hides his money in the ground—wasn't there a danger that people would miss his religious meaning? Would it be enough simply to tell a story about ordinary people living in an everyday world of vineyard tending and housekeeping, and then let the listener or reader scramble for meaning? Often, it would seem, they decided it was not. And so the gospeller tells us what the wheat and the tares signify, explicates exactly who was meant to be understood by the seed that fell on dry and stony ground. Two thousand years of commentary and preaching have turned the "minimalist" narratives of Jesus into venerable Christian teaching. But what would it be like to hear one of the parables for the first time, just on its own?

Or, to put the question another way, what if you were to open up the latest *New Yorker* magazine and find, in this week's fiction offering, a story about a father and two sons? Imagine your reading experience to be something like the following, that is, less a "reception of the gospel" proclaimed in church and more the reading of a story without preconception, in ignorance of where the author "stands." It begins with a shocker: the younger of the two brothers asking for his inheritance prematurely, before his father's death. Then, against your readerly expectations, not to mention your actual experience of parents and money, the father decides immediately to grant this request straightaway. The windfall, however, does not start the young man in careful investment or a career in real estate; instead it launches him in ruin. Somehow the young man's downward spiral does not come as a surprise. Nor does his decision to return home, where even under the worst circumstances of guilt and embarrassment he can at least expect to receive regular meals and not to pay rent. But what the son is not prepared for is what, in fact, also takes you aback. For rather than allowing the drama of the scene to build toward a major confession of regret and resolve, the storyteller shifts attention away from the son and to the father, who interrupts the youth's analysis of what went wrong with an outpouring of generosity no one would have expected. Presents are lavished and a party is arranged. But then the whole situation is put in the most extreme terms, as if what were at stake here were more than could meet the eye: "for this son of mine was dead and is alive again; he was lost and is found!" (Luke 15:24).

It is not clear why the story doesn't end there, but it does not. Instead, focus shifts once again, this time to the elder son who was lost sight of after the opening scene. He is clearly another type altogether, as earnest and diligent as his brother is irresponsible. He is also filled with rage when he learns of the fuss being made over the "prodigal" who's come home. He notes the gifts he has not received, the living he has not wasted; but most of all, he registers the injustice of the homecoming's festivity, the sheer offense of the father's welcome for a brother he can refer to only as "this son of *yours*." You note how the outrage is being meted out and you think the father is well within his rights to send the naysayer to his room. Instead, however, he opens up a door between himself and the elder brother. He calls him "son," reminds him not only of the constancy of their unbroken relationship but of the full extent of the inheritance that awaits him alone ("all that is mine is yours"). In the end, the father once again insists on the importance of joy, on remembering the stakes that are highest of all— life and death, loss and recovery.

Taken out of the Gospel of Luke, separated from the other parables of lost sheep and lost coin, viewed apart from Jesus's controversy with the Pharisees and apart even from his identity as the Son of God—in short, taken only on its own, with no more authority than what comes, say, with publication in the *New Yorker*—what is it that the story gives us? On the simplest level, it is a domestic tale of father and sons, of a single parent family and sibling rivalry. The sons are predictable enough, the night and day contrasts you recognize both from fiction and from life. But it is the father who proves remarkable. You think of his lack of interest in hearing the younger son's apology, his patience with the elder's complaints, the way he refuses to deal with anything less than the biggest picture—life and death, loss and recovery.

Interpretation does not stop there, however. Given the whole range of issues that feminist criticism has taught us to notice, for instance, you begin to see other things as well. There is the absence of the mother and the extraordinary degree to which the patriarch of this family story seems to embody so many of the values we identify as matriarchal or feminine. In addition to what might be called gender issues, there is also a great deal that has to do with material culture. Marxist critics have reminded us of the importance of economic realities in any fictional world. And so you notice the ways they are played out here: practices with regard to inheritance, the importance of the elder son's unique status, the significance of luxury objects (like rings, and shoes, and fatted calves), the way possessions broker position and confer status.

But after allowing yourself to experience the story in all these different ways, is there anything about it that argues the necessary presence of what Flannery O'Connor spoke of as the "added dimension"? Is there reason to treat this human drama as more than another family narrative or to connect it to the mystery of our life in God? Is there any warrant for reading it as Christian and therefore as worthy of inclusion in a church's adult education?

If the story were not a parable told by Jesus and preached to the faithful over the course of the last two thousand years, the answer might well be No. For rather than talking about grace, let alone explaining how God saves us, the story operates indirectly and at a remove; rather than giving us examples of transformed human lives, it describes situations in which transformation is as yet only a possibility. One looks in vain for a moral or even for a religious resolution. Instead, gestures are made to speak louder than words, as the father first runs in love toward the one son who simply comes home and then leaves a party to find the other one who will not stop working. So much is left unsaid, or, if spoken, then hidden in the depths of words like *dead* and *alive, lost* and *found.* Heaven is but mentioned in passing and the name of God not at all. In other words, you are left with an experience to interpret, a few clues, and no answers.

And yet what might happen if a group of Christians read this story together? Our hope is that people gathering around the fiction and essays included in this resource will take the occasion to listen for God in new places. There is no telling, of course, where one may hear the Word spoken; it has been said that even the stones will cry it out. The hope of this curriculum, in any event, is that the selections chosen here will raise questions, spark discussion, make the life of faith more an engagement with contemporary American culture and less a flight from it.

O'Connor, Carver, and Walker all write short stories that culminate in revelation, with each one leaving the reader to decide what it is that has been revealed. Buechner, Hampl, and Rodriguez explore the possibility of memoir as a kind of spiritual pilgrimage, an autobiographical search that leads them beyond themselves. Annie Dillard's essays reflect on all that nature opens up about the mystery of God and all that it conceals. Finally, Garrison Keillor reminds us that humor keeps the life of faith honest by also keeping it humble and generous. Our hope is to show that while contemporary American literature may not be the most predictable place to listen for God, it may well turn out to be among the most rewarding.

Peter S. Hawkins

Notes

1. *Collected Works of Flannery O'Connor* (New York: Library of America, distributed by Viking Press, 1988), 804-805.

2. *Conversations with Raymond Carver*, eds. Marshall Bruce Gentry and William L. Stull (Jackson: University Press of Mississippi, 1990), 46.

3. *Collected Works*, 940.

4. Patricia Hampl, *Virgin Time* (New York: Farrar, Straus & Giroux, 1992), 175.

Flannery O'Connor

Less than thirty years after her death in 1964, Flannery O'Connor was included in the prestigious "Library of America" and thereby ranked with the likes of Nathaniel Hawthorne and Henry James. During her lifetime, however, she despaired of being understood by more than a few. Contemporary reviewers were dismayed by what they saw as her propensity for writing "horror stories." Considering plot lines alone, it is easy to see why. In *Wise Blood*, the first of her two novels, a backwoods evangelist of "The Church Without Christ" blinds himself with lye and fills his shoes with crushed glass. In "Greenleaf" a farm woman is gored by a bull, in "A Good Man Is Hard to Find" a grandmother is shot in cold blood by an escaped convict, and in "Good Country People" a would-be philosopher of Nihilism has her wooden leg stolen by a supposedly innocent Bible salesman. O'Connor readily conceded her use of violence, the presence of "freaks," even the place of horror in her work; she knew very well that the world of her fiction was "hard." But there was also an "added dimension" of faith that was the key to her writing. She wrote the way she did, she told a friend, precisely because she was a Christian, and "there is nothing harder or less sentimental than Christian realism."[1]

By "realism" O'Connor did not mean an obligation to what passes for normal. Rather, she was interested in portraying human reality as she saw it from the perspective of her Catholic faith—as fallen, judged, and redeemed. To present the world as if it were not broken, not enthralled by the devil, would be to tell a lie; but so too would be any presentation of it as absurd and meaningless, cut off from the power of God. The task of the Christian realist, therefore, was to describe the world through the eyes of faith, to show it held fast in the grip of evil but constantly assaulted by God's grace.

With some notable exceptions, O'Connor's characters are neither notorious sinners nor openly of the devil's party. She herself described them as poor, afflicted both in body and mind, with little sense of spiritual purpose. And yet this bare sketch in no way gives a sense of the vital presence of her "people": spoiled intellectuals reluctantly living at home with their well-meaning but overbearing mothers; know-it-alls dedicated to teaching everyone else a lesson; rural Southerners who are Christ-haunted, if not Christ-centered. Nor does summary or paraphrase give any sense of her humor.

In one sense, O'Connor's fictional world is narrow. It is a rural South of small beleaguered landowners and their hired hands, of mothers who "cope" with life and their educated but maladjusted children who do not. She has a superb eye for dialogue and detail, a gift for conjuring up the particular "manners" that evoke an entire social landscape. The thrust of her fiction, however, is to move from manners to mystery, from a humorous presentation of business as usual to a dramatic reassessment of everything.

Typically a story will begin by showing someone in apparent if uneasy control, locked tight in a universe of his or her own making, defended against change. Inevitably, however, change arrives on the scene and with it the shattering of worlds. Some stories culminate in a breakdown, a cataclysm that leaves no sense of what may follow upon devastation; in others she suggests how breakdown may also be a breaking through. Sometimes this can lead to a major epiphany, where the tone of the narrative heightens into the sublime and a character is able to see into the spiritual heart of things (as in "The Artificial Nigger," "Revelation," "Temple of the Holy Ghost"). More often, however, insight is only fragmentary, more implied by the narrator than ever grasped by the characters themselves. "All my stories," she wrote, "are about the action of grace on a character who is not very willing to support it. . . ."[2] This "action of grace" usually falls like a ton of bricks on people who have not heeded the warning signs, as if nothing less than some radical gesture—a gun pointed to the head, a fire in the woods, or, literally, the loss of a leg to stand on—can grab their attention. Likewise, those who act as agents of grace most often do so unwittingly, even against their characters and wills. O'Connor believed that God uses the imperfect and banal, even the outright evil, to work the divine will. Therefore, hypocritical grandmothers, devious Bible salesmen, and malicious boys can all, quite despite themselves, serve as the Lord's ministers.

All of these themes appear in "Revelation," a story O'Connor finished revising shortly before her death of lupus at the age of thirty-nine. The protagonist, Mrs. Turpin, is perhaps her finest realization of a type familiar elsewhere in her work. She is the commanding presence of a little world, who sizes up every situation (be it a doctor's waiting room or society at large) and confidently judges the worth of all. Invariably, she finds herself the winner. In the first half of the narrative O'Connor brings the action to a steady boil precisely as Mrs. Turpin makes her judgments, forges her alliances, and never fails to give credit where it is due—to the God who made her exactly as she is: "Thank you, Jesus, for making everything the way it is!"

As this self-congratulation builds to a crescendo, we notice the steady antagonism of a college girl, Mary Grace, who throughout the first half of the story has been glaring at Mrs. Turpin with unconcealed loathing. When she can take no more of the hypocrisy she throws a book (entitled, *Human Development!*) at Mrs. Turpin that not only sets the woman reeling but that precipitates everything that follows. Face to face with her assailant, Mrs. Turpin demands to know why she has been singled out. " 'What you got to say to me?' she asked hoarsely and held her breath, waiting, as for a revelation." When the girl answers, it is more than Mrs Turpin bargained on: "Go back to hell where you came from, you old wart hog." For the rest of the story she lives with this furious oracle, until, overcome with rage and frustration, she hurls her outrage at God. "A final surge of fury shook her and she roared, 'Who do you think you are?' "

This attack on the Almighty then echoes back on her, so that she hears her own words to God as if addressed to herself. O'Connor does not fully explain what happens next, as Mrs. Turpin realizes her finitude, the fragility of her world, and the "very heart of mystery" that pulses with life. From the wreckage of her self-esteem, however, she turns to behold a vision she would never have been capable of before. As at the outset of the story, she judges everyone; even in this moment of transcendence she is transfixed by hierarchy, by the certitude of there being a bottom and a top. And yet what she beholds is a profound reversal of all that had once been in place: the last are now first and the first last. O'Connor tells us neither what Mrs.Turpin will finally make of this vision nor who she will become. But the story's last word is "hallelujah."

Peter S. Hawkins

Notes

1. *Collected Works of Flannery O'Connor*, ed. Sally Fitzgerald (New York: Library of America, distributed by Viking Press, 1988), 942.

2. *Collected Works*, 1067.

Revelation

The doctor's waiting room, which was very small, was almost full when the Turpins entered and Mrs. Turpin, who was very large, made it look even smaller by her presence. She stood looming at the head of the magazine table set in the center of it, a living demonstration that the room was inadequate and ridiculous. Her little bright black eyes took in all the patients as she sized up the seating situation. There was one vacant chair and a place on the sofa occupied by a blond child in a dirty blue romper who should have been told to move over and make room for the lady. He was five or six, but Mrs. Turpin saw at once that no one was going to tell him to move over. He was slumped down in the seat, his arms idle at his sides and his eyes idle in his head; his nose ran unchecked.

Mrs. Turpin put a firm hand on Claud's shoulder and said in a voice that included anyone who wanted to listen, "Claud, you sit in that chair there," and gave him a push down into the vacant one. Claud was florid and bald and sturdy, somewhat shorter than Mrs. Turpin, but he sat down as if he were accustomed to doing what she told him to.

Mrs. Turpin remained standing. The only man in the room besides Claud was a lean stringy old fellow with a rusty hand spread out on each knee, whose eyes were closed as if he were asleep or dead or pretending to be so as not to get up and offer her his seat. Her gaze settled agreeably on a well-dressed gray-haired lady whose eyes met hers and whose expression said: if that child belonged to me, he would have some manners and move over—there's plenty of room there for you and him too.

Claud looked up with a sigh and made as if to rise.

"Sit down," Mrs. Turpin said. "You know you're not supposed to stand on that leg. He has an ulcer on his leg," she explained.

Claud lifted his foot onto the magazine table and rolled his trouser leg up to reveal a purple swelling on a plump marble-white calf.

"My!" the pleasant lady said. "How did you do that?"

"A cow kicked him," Mrs. Turpin said.

"Goodness!" said the lady.

Claud rolled his trouser leg down.

"Maybe the little boy would move over," the lady suggested, but the child did not stir.

"Somebody will be leaving in a minute," Mrs. Turpin said. She could not understand why a doctor—with as much money as they made charging five dollars a day to just stick their head in the hospital door and look at you—couldn't afford a decent-sized waiting room. This one was hardly bigger than a garage. The table was cluttered with limp-looking magazines and at one end of it there was a big green glass ash tray full of cigarette butts and cotton wads with little blood spots on them. If she had had anything to do with the running of the place, that would have been emptied every so often. There were no chairs against the wall at the head of the room. It had a rectangular-shaped panel in it that permitted a view of the office where the nurse came and went and the secretary listened to the radio. A plastic fern in a gold pot sat in the opening and trailed its fronds down almost to the floor. The radio was softly playing gospel music.

Just then the inner door opened and a nurse with the highest stack of yellow hair Mrs. Turpin had ever seen put her face in the crack and called for the next patient. The woman sitting beside Claud grasped the two arms of her chair and hoisted herself up; she pulled her dress free from her legs and lumbered through the door where the nurse had disappeared.

Mrs. Turpin eased into the vacant chair, which held her tight as a corset. "I wish I could reduce," she said, and rolled her eyes and gave a comic sigh.

"Oh, you aren't fat," the stylish lady said.

"Ooooo I am too," Mrs. Turpin said. "Claud he eats all he wants to and never weighs over one hundred and seventy-five pounds, but me I just look at something good to eat and I gain some weight," and her stomach and shoulders shook with laughter. "You can eat all you want to, can't you, Claud?" she asked, turning to him.

Claud only grinned.

"Well, as long as you have such a good disposition," the stylish lady said, "I don't think it makes a bit of difference what size you are. You just can't beat a good disposition."

Next to her was a fat girl of eighteen or nineteen, scowling into a thick blue book which Mrs. Turpin saw was entitled *Human Development*. The girl raised her head and directed her scowl at Mrs. Turpin as if she did not like her looks. She appeared annoyed that anyone should speak while she tried to read. The poor girl's face was blue with acne and Mrs. Turpin thought how pitiful it was to have a face like that at that age. She gave the girl a friendly smile but the girl only scowled the harder. Mrs. Turpin herself was fat but she had always had good skin, and, though she was forty-seven years old, there was not a wrinkle in her face except around her eyes from laughing too much.

Next to the ugly girl was the child, still in exactly the same position, and next to him was a thin leathery old woman in a cotton print dress. She and Claud had three sacks of chicken feed in their pump house that was in the same print. She had seen from the first that the child belonged with the old woman. She could tell by the way they sat—kind of vacant and white-trashy, as if they would sit there until Doomsday if nobody called and told them to get up. And at right angles but next to the well-dressed pleasant lady was a lank-faced woman who was certainly the child's mother. She had on a yellow sweat shirt and wine-colored slacks, both gritty-looking, and the rims of her lips were stained with snuff. Her dirty yellow hair was tied behind with a little piece of red paper ribbon. Worse than niggers any day, Mrs. Turpin thought.

The gospel hymn playing was, "When I looked up and He looked down," and Mrs. Turpin, who knew it, supplied the last line mentally, "And wona these days I know I'll we-eara crown."

Without appearing to, Mrs. Turpin always noticed people's feet. The well-dressed lady had on red and gray suede shoes to match her dress. Mrs. Turpin had on her good black patent leather pumps. The ugly girl had on Girl Scout shoes and heavy socks. The old woman had on tennis shoes and the white-trashy mother had on what appeared to be bedroom slippers, black straw with gold braid threaded through them—exactly what you would have expected her to have on.

Sometimes at night when she couldn't go to sleep, Mrs. Turpin would occupy herself with the question of who she would have chosen to be if she couldn't have been herself. If Jesus had said to her before he made her, "There's only two places available for you. You can either be a nigger or white-trash," what would she have said? "Please, Jesus, please," she would have said, "just let me wait until there's another place available," and he would have said, "No, you have to go right now and I have only those two places so make up your mind." She would have wiggled and squirmed and begged and pleaded but it would have been no use and finally she would have said, "All right, make me a nigger then—but that don't mean a trashy one." And he would have made her a neat clean respectable Negro woman, herself but black.

Next to the child's mother was a red-headed youngish woman, reading one of the magazines and working a piece of chewing gum, hell for leather, as Claud would say. Mrs. Turpin could not see the woman's feet. She was not white-trash, just common. Sometimes Mrs. Turpin occupied herself at night naming the classes of people. On the bottom of the heap were most colored people, not the kind she would have been if she had been one, but most of them; then next to them—not above, just away from—were the white-trash; then above them were the home-owners, and above them the home-and-land owners, to which she and Claud belonged. Above she and Claud were people with a lot of money and much bigger houses and much more land. But here the complexity of it would begin to bear in on her, for some of the people with a lot money were common and ought to be below she and Claud and some of the people who had good blood had lost their money and had to rent and then there were colored people who owned their homes and land as well. There was a colored dentist in town who had two red Lincolns and a swimming pool and a farm with registered white-face cattle on it. Usually by the time she had fallen asleep all the classes of people were moiling and roiling around in her head, and she would dream they were all crammed in together in a box car, being ridden off to be put in a gas oven.

"That's a beautiful clock," she said and nodded to her right. It was a big wall clock, the face encased in a brass sunburst.

"Yes, it's very pretty," the stylish lady said agreeably. "And right on the dot too," she added, glancing at her watch.

The ugly girl beside her cast an eye upward at the clock, smirked, then looked directly at Mrs. Turpin and smirked again. Then she returned her eyes to her book. She was obviously the lady's daughter because, although they didn't look anything alike as to disposition, they both had the same shape of face and the same blue eyes. On the lady they sparkled pleasantly but in the girl's seared face they appeared alternately to smolder and to blaze.

What if Jesus had said, "All right, you can be white-trash or a nigger or ugly"!

Mrs. Turpin felt an awful pity for the girl, though she thought it was one thing to be ugly and another to act ugly.

The woman with the snuff-stained lips turned around in her chair and looked up at the clock. Then she turned back and appeared to look a little to the side of Mrs. Turpin. There was a cast in one of her eyes. "You want to know wher you can get you one of themther clocks?" she asked in a loud voice.

"No, I already have a nice clock," Mrs. Turpin said. Once somebody like her got a leg in the conversation, she would be all over it.

"You can get you one with green stamps," the woman said. "That's most likely wher he got hisn. Save you up enough, you can get you most anythang. I got me some joo'ry."

Ought to have got you a wash rag and some soap, Mrs. Turpin thought.

"I get contour sheets with mine," the pleasant lady said.

The daughter slammed her book shut. She looked straight in front of her, directly through Mrs. Turpin and on through the yellow curtain and the plate glass window which made the wall behind her. The girl's eyes seemed lit all of a sudden with a peculiar light, an unnatural light like night road signs give. Mrs. Turpin turned her head to see if there was anything going on outside that she should see, but she could not see anything. Figures passing cast only a pale shadow through the curtain. There was no reason the girl should single her out for her ugly looks.

"Miss Finley," the nurse said, cracking the door. The gum-chewing woman got up and passed in front of her and Claud and went into the office. She had on red high-heeled shoes.

Directly across the table, the ugly girl's eyes were fixed on Mrs. Turpin as if she had some very special reason for disliking her.

"This is wonderful weather, isn't it?" the girl's mother said.

"It's good weather for cotton if you can get the niggers to pick it," Mrs. Turpin said, "but niggers don't want to pick cotton any more. You can't get the white folks to pick it and now you can't get the niggers—because they got to be right up there with the white folks."

"They gonna *try* anyways," the white-trash woman said, leaning forward.

"Do you have one of the cotton-picking machines?" the pleasant lady asked.

"No," Mrs. Turpin said, "they leave half the cotton in the field. We don't have much cotton anyway. If you want to make it farming now, you have to have a little of everything. We got a couple of acres of cotton and a few hogs and chickens and just enough white-face that Claud can look after them himself."

"One thang I don't want," the white-trash woman said, wiping her mouth with the back of her hand. "Hogs. Nasty stinking things, a-gruntin and a-rootin all over the place."

Mrs. Turpin gave her the merest edge of her attention. "Our hogs are not dirty and they don't stink," she said. "They're cleaner than some children I've seen. Their feet never touch the ground. We have a pig-parlor—that's where you raise them on concrete," she explained to the pleasant lady, "and Claud scoots them down with the hose every afternoon and washes off the floor." Cleaner by far than that child right there, she thought. Poor nasty little thing. He had not moved except to put the thumb of his dirty hand into his mouth.

The woman turned her face away from Mrs. Turpin. "I know I wouldn't scoot down no hog with no hose," she said to the wall.

You wouldn't have no hog to scoot down, Mrs. Turpin said to herself.

"A-gruntin and a-rootin and a-groanin," the woman muttered.

"We got a little of everything," Mrs. Turpin said to the pleasant lady. "It's no use in having more than you can handle yourself with help like it is. We found enough niggers to pick our cotton this year but Claud he has to go after them and take them home again in the evening. They can't walk that half a mile. No they can't. I tell you," she said and laughed merrily, "I sure am tired of buttering up niggers, but you got to love em if you want em to work for you. When they come in the morning, I run out and I say, 'Hi yawl this morning?' and when Claud drives them off to the field I just wave to beat the band and they just wave back." And she waved her hand rapidly to illustrate.

"Like you read out of the same book," the lady said, showing she understood perfectly.

"Child, yes," Mrs. Turpin said. "And when they come in from the field, I run out with a bucket of icewater. That's the way it's going to be from now on," she said. "You may as well face it."

"One thang I know," the white-trash woman said. "Two thangs I ain't going to do: love no niggers or scoot down no hog with no hose." And she let out a bark of contempt.

The look that Mrs. Turpin and the pleasant lady exchanged indicated they both understood that you had to *have* certain things before you could *know* certain things. But every time Mrs. Turpin exchanged a look with the lady, she was aware that the ugly girl's peculiar eyes were still on her, and she had trouble bringing her attention back to the conversation.

"When you got something," she said, "you got to look after it." And when you ain't got a thing but breath and britches, she added to herself, you can afford to come to town every morning and just sit on the Court House coping and spit.

A grotesque revolving shadow passed across the curtain behind her and was thrown palely on the opposite wall. Then a bicycle clattered down against the outside of the building. The door opened and a colored boy glided in with a tray from the drugstore. It had two large red and white paper cups on it with tops on them. He was a tall, very black boy in discolored white pants and a green nylon shirt. He was chewing gum slowly, as if to music. He set the tray down in the office opening next to the fern and stuck his head through to look for the secretary. She was not in there. He rested his arms on the ledge and waited, his narrow bottom stuck out, swaying to the left and right. He raised a hand over his head and scratched the base of his skull.

"You see that button there, boy?" Mrs. Turpin said. "You can punch that and she'll come. She's probably in the back somewhere."

"Is thas right?" the boy said agreeably, as if he had never seen the button before. He leaned to the right and put his finger on it. "She sometime out," he said and twisted around to face his audience, his elbows behind him on the counter. The nurse appeared and he twisted back again. She handed him a dollar and he rooted in his pocket and made the change and counted it out to her. She gave him fifteen cents for a tip and he went out with the empty tray. The heavy door swung to slowly and closed at length with the sound of suction. For a moment no one spoke.

"They ought to send all them niggers back to Africa," the white-trash woman said. "That's wher they come from in the first place."

"Oh, I couldn't do without my good colored friends," the pleasant lady said.

"There's a heap of things worse than a nigger," Mrs. Turpin agreed. "It's all kinds of them just like it's all kinds of us."

"Yes, and it takes all kinds to make the world go round," the lady said in her musical voice.

As she said it, the raw-complexioned girl snapped her teeth together. Her lower lip turned downwards and inside out, revealing the pale pink inside of her mouth. After a second it rolled back up. It was the ugliest face Mrs. Turpin had ever seen anyone make and for a moment she was certain that the girl had made it at her. She was looking at her as if she had known and disliked her all her life—all of Mrs. Turpin's life, it seemed too, not just all the girl's life. Why, girl, I don't even know you, Mrs. Turpin said silently.

She forced her attention back to the discussion. "It wouldn't be practical to send them back to Africa," she said. "They wouldn't want to go. They got it too good here."

"Wouldn't be what they wanted—if I had anythang to do with it," the woman said.

"It wouldn't be a way in the world you could get all the niggers back over there," Mrs. Turpin said. "They'd be hiding out and lying down and turning sick on you and wailing and hollering and raring and pitching. It wouldn't be a way in the world to get them over there."

"They got over here," the trashy woman said. "Get back like they got over."

"It wasn't so many of them then," Mrs. Turpin explained.

The woman looked at Mrs. Turpin as if here was an idiot indeed but Mrs. Turpin was not bothered by the look, considering where it came from.

"Nooo," she said, "they're going to stay here where they can go to New York and marry white folks and improve their color. That's what they all want to do, every one of them, improve their color."

"You know what comes of that, don't you?" Claud asked.

"No, Claud, what?" Mrs. Turpin said.

Claud's eyes twinkled. "White-faced niggers," he said with never a smile.

Everybody in the office laughed except the white-trash and the ugly girl. The girl gripped the book in her lap with white fingers. The trashy woman looked around her from face to face as if she thought they were all idiots. The old woman in the feed sack dress continued to gaze expressionless across the floor at the high-top shoes of the man opposite her, the one who had been pretending to be asleep when the Turpins came in. He was laughing heartily, his hands still spread out on his knees. The child had fallen to the side and was lying now almost face down in the old woman's lap.

While they recovered from their laughter, the nasal chorus on the radio kept the room from silence.

> "You go to blank blank,
> And I'll go to mine
> But we'll all blank along
> To-geth-ther,
> And all along the blank
> We'll hep each other out
> Smile-ling in any kind of
> Weath-ther!"

Mrs. Turpin didn't catch every word but she caught enough to agree with the spirit of the song and it turned her thoughts sober. To help anybody out that needed it was her philosophy of life. She never spared herself when she found somebody in need, whether they were white or black, trash or decent. And of all she had to be thankful for, she was most thankful that this was so. If Jesus had said, "You can be high society and have all the money you want and be thin and svelte-like, but you can't be a good woman with it," she would have had to say, "Well don't make me that then. Make me a good woman and it don't matter what else, how fat or how ugly or how poor!" Her heart rose. He had not made her a nigger or white-trash or ugly! He had made her herself and given her a little of everything. Jesus, thank you! she said. Thank you thank you thank you! Whenever she counted her blessings she felt as buoyant as if she weighed one hundred and twenty-five pounds instead of one hundred and eighty.

"What's wrong with your little boy?" the pleasant lady asked the white-trashy woman.

"He has a ulcer," the woman said proudly. "He ain't give me a minute's peace since he was born. Him and her are just alike," she said, nodding at the old woman, who was running her leathery fingers through the child's pale hair. "Look like I can't get nothing down them two but Co'Cola and candy."

That's all you try to get down em, Mrs. Turpin said to herself. Too lazy to light the fire. There was nothing you could tell her about people like them that she didn't know already. And it was not just that they didn't have anything. Because if you gave them everything, in two weeks it would all be broken or filthy or they would have chopped it all for lightwood. She knew all this from her own experience. Help them you must, but help them you couldn't.

All at once the ugly girl turned her lips inside out again. Her eyes fixed like two drills on Mrs. Turpin. This time there was no mistaking that there was something urgent behind them.

Girl, Mrs. Turpin exclaimed silently, I haven't done a thing to you! The girl might be confusing her with somebody else. There was no need to sit by and let herself be intimidated. "You must be in college," she said boldly, looking directly at the girl. "I see you reading a book there."

The girl continued to stare and pointedly did not answer.

Her mother blushed at this rudeness. "The lady asked you a question, Mary Grace," she said under her breath.

"I have ears," Mary Grace said.

The poor mother blushed again. "Mary Grace goes to Wellesley College," she explained. She twisted one of the buttons on her dress. "In Massachusetts," she added with a grimace. "And in the summer she just keeps right on studying. Just reads all the time, a real book worm. She's done real well at Wellesley; she's taking English and Math and History and Psychology and Social Studies," she rattled on, "and I think it's too much. I think she ought to get out and have fun."

The girl looked as if she would like to hurl them all through the plate glass window.

"Way up north," Mrs. Turpin murmured and thought, well, it hasn't done much for her manners.

"I'd almost rather to have him sick," the white-trash woman said, wrenching the attention back to herself. "He's so mean when he ain't. Look like some children just take natural to meanness. It's some gets bad when they get sick but he was the opposite. Took sick and turned good. He don't give me no trouble now. It's me waitin to see the doctor," she said.

If I was going to send anybody back to Africa, Mrs. Turpin thought, it would be your kind, woman. "Yes, indeed," she said aloud, but looking up at the ceiling, "it's a heap of things worse than a nigger." And dirtier than a hog, she added to herself.

"I think people with bad dispositions are more to be pitied than anyone on earth," the pleasant lady said in a voice that was decidedly thin.

"I thank the Lord he has blessed me with a good one," Mrs. Turpin said. "The day has never dawned that I couldn't find something to laugh at."

"Not since she married me anyways," Claud said with a comical straight face.

Everybody laughed except the girl and the white-trash.

Mrs. Turpin's stomach shook. "He's such a caution," she said, "that I can't help but laugh at him."

The girl made a loud ugly noise through her teeth.

Her mother's mouth grew thin and tight. "I think the worst thing in the world," she said, "is an ungrateful person. To have everything and not appreciate it. I know a girl," she said, "who has parents who would give her anything, a little brother who loves her dearly, who is getting a good education, who wears the best clothes, but who can never say a kind word to anyone, who never smiles, who just criticizes and complains all day long."

"Is she too old to paddle?" Claud asked.

The girl's face was almost purple.

"Yes," the lady said, "I'm afraid there's nothing to do but leave her to her folly. Some day she'll wake up and it'll be too late."

"It never hurt anyone to smile," Mrs. Turpin said. "It just makes you feel better all over."

"Of course," the lady said sadly, "but there are just some people you can't tell anything to. They can't take criticism."

"If it's one thing I am," Mrs. Turpin said with feeling, "it's grateful. When I think who all I could have been besides myself and what all I got, a little of everything, and a good disposition besides, I just feel like shouting, 'Thank you, Jesus, for making everything the way it is!' It could have been different!" For one thing, somebody else could have got Claud. At the thought of this, she was flooded with gratitude and a terrible pang of joy ran through her. "Oh thank you, Jesus, Jesus, thank you!" she cried aloud.

The book struck her directly over her left eye. It struck almost at the same instant that she realized the girl was about to hurl it. Before she could utter a sound, the raw face came crashing across the table toward her, howling. The girl's fingers sank like clamps into the soft flesh of her neck. She heard the mother cry out and Claud shout, "Whoa!" There was an instant when she was certain that she was about to be in an earthquake.

All at once her vision narrowed and she saw everything as if it were happening in a small room far away, or as if she were looking at it through the wrong end of a telescope. Claud's face crumpled and fell out of sight. The nurse ran in, then out, then in again. Then the gangling figure of the doctor rushed out of the inner door. Magazines flew this way and that as the table turned over. The girl fell with a thud and Mrs. Turpin's vision suddenly reversed itself and she saw everything large instead of small. The eyes of the white-trashy woman were staring hugely at the floor. There the girl, held down on one side by the nurse and on the other by her mother, was wrenching and turning in their grasp. The doctor was kneeling astride her, trying to hold her arm down. He managed after a second to sink a long needle into it.

Mrs. Turpin felt entirely hollow except for her heart which swung from side to side as if it were agitated in a great empty drum of flesh.

"Somebody that's not busy call for the ambulance," the doctor said in the off-hand voice young doctors adopt for terrible occasions.

Mrs. Turpin could not have moved a finger. The old man who had been sitting next to her skipped nimbly into the office and made the call, for the secretary still seemed to be gone.

"Claud!" Mrs. Turpin called.

He was not in his chair. She knew she must jump up and find him but she felt like some one trying to catch a tram in a dream, when everything moves in slow motion and the faster you try to run the slower you go.

"Here I am," a suffocated voice, very unlike Claud's, said.

He was doubled up in the corner on the floor, pale as paper, holding his leg. She wanted to get up and go to him but she could not move. Instead, her gaze was drawn slowly downward to the churning face on the floor, which she could see over the doctor's shoulder.

The girl's eyes stopped rolling and focused on her. They seemed a much lighter blue than before, as if a door that had been tightly closed behind them was now open to admit light and air.

Mrs. Turpin's head cleared and her power of motion returned. She leaned forward until she was looking directly into the fierce brilliant eyes. There was no doubt in her mind that the girl did know her, knew her in some intense and personal way, beyond time and place and condition. "What you got to say to me?" she asked hoarsely and held her breath, waiting, as for a revelation.

The girl raised her head. Her gaze locked with Mrs. Turpin's. "Go back to hell where you came from, you old wart hog," she whispered. Her voice was low but clear. Her eyes burned for a moment as if she saw with pleasure that her message had struck its target.

Mrs. Turpin sank back in her chair.

After a moment the girl's eyes closed and she turned her head wearily to the side.

The doctor rose and handed the nurse the empty syringe. He leaned over and put both hands for a moment on the mother's shoulders, which were shaking. She was sitting on the floor, her lips pressed together, holding Mary Grace's hand in her lap. The girl's fingers were gripped like a baby's around her thumb. "Go on to the hospital," he said. "I'll call and make the arrangements."

"Now let's see that neck," he said in a jovial voice to Mrs. Turpin.

He began to inspect her neck with his first two fingers. Two little moon-shaped lines like pink fish bones were indented over her windpipe. There was the beginning of an angry red swelling above her eye. His fingers passed over this also.

"Lea' me be," she said thickly and shook him off. "See about Claud. She kicked him."

"I'll see about him in a minute," he said and felt her pulse. He was a thin gray-haired man, given to pleasantries. "Go home and have yourself a vacation the rest of the day," he said and patted her on the shoulder.

Quit your pattin me, Mrs. Turpin growled to herself.

"And put an ice pack over that eye," he said. Then he went and squatted down beside Claud and looked at his leg. After a moment he pulled him up and Claud limped after him into the office.

Until the ambulance came, the only sounds in the room were the tremulous moans of the girl's mother, who continued to sit on the floor. The white-trash woman did not take her eyes off the girl. Mrs. Turpin looked straight ahead at nothing. Presently the ambulance drew up, a long dark shadow, behind the curtain. The attendants came in and set the stretcher down beside the girl and lifted her expertly onto it and carried her out. The nurse helped the mother gather up her things. The shadow of the ambulance moved silently away and the nurse came back in the office.

"That ther girl is going to be a lunatic, ain't she?" the white-trash woman asked the nurse, but the nurse kept on to the back and never answered her.

"Yes, she's going to be a lunatic," the white-trash woman said to the rest of them.

"Po' critter," the old woman murmured. The child's face was still in her lap. His eyes looked idly out over her knees. He had not moved during the disturbance except to draw one leg up under him.

"I thank Gawd," the white-trash woman said fervently, "I ain't a lunatic."

Claud came limping out and the Turpins went home.

As their pick-up truck turned into their own dirt road and made the crest of the hill, Mrs. Turpin gripped the window ledge and looked out suspiciously. The land sloped gracefully down through a field dotted with lavender weeds and at the start of the rise their small yellow frame house, with its little flower beds spread out around it like a fancy apron, sat primly in its accustomed place between two giant hickory trees. She would not have been startled to see a burnt wound between two blackened chimneys.

Neither of them felt like eating so they put on their house clothes and lowered the shade in the bedroom and lay down, Claud with his leg on a pillow and herself with a damp washcloth over her eye. The instant she was flat on her back, the image of a razor-backed hog with warts on its face and horns coming out behind its ears snorted into her head. She moaned, a low quiet moan.

"I am not," she said tearfully, "a wart hog. From hell." But the denial had no force. The girl's eyes and her words, even the tone of her voice, low but clear, directed only to her, brooked no repudiation. She had been singled out for the message, though there was trash in the room to whom it might justly have been applied. The full force of this fact struck her only now. There was a woman there who was neglecting her own child but she had been overlooked. The message had been given to Ruby Turpin, a respectable, hard-working, church-going woman. The tears dried. Her eyes began to burn instead with wrath.

She rose on her elbow and the washcloth fell into her hand. Claud was lying on his back, snoring. She wanted to tell him what the girl had said. At the same time, she did not wish to put the image of herself as a wart hog from hell into his mind.

"Hey, Claud," she muttered and pushed his shoulder.

Claud opened one pale baby blue eye.

She looked into it warily. He did not think about anything. He just went his way.

"Wha, whasit?" he said and closed the eye again.

"Nothing," she said. "Does your leg pain you?"

"Hurts like hell," Claud said.

"It'll quit terreckly," she said and lay back down. In a moment Claud was snoring again. For the rest of the afternoon they lay there. Claud slept. She scowled at the ceiling. Occasionally she raised her fist and made a small stabbing motion over her chest as if she was defending her innocence to invisible guests who were like the comforters of Job, reasonable-seeming but wrong.

About five-thirty Claud stirred. "Got to go after those niggers," he sighed, not moving.

She was looking straight up as if there were unintelligible handwriting on the ceiling. The protuberance over her eye had turned a greenish-blue. "Listen here," she said.

"What?"

"Kiss me."

Claud leaned over and kissed her loudly on the mouth. He pinched her side and their hands interlocked. Her expression of ferocious concentration did not change. Claud got up, groaning and growling, and limped off. She continued to study the ceiling.

She did not get up until she heard the pick-up truck coming back with the Negroes. Then she rose and thrust her feet in her brown oxfords, which she did not bother to lace, and stumped out onto the back porch and got her red plastic bucket. She emptied a tray of ice cubes into it and filled it half full of water and went out into the back yard. Every afternoon after Claud brought the hands in, one of the boys helped him put out hay and the rest waited in the back of the truck until he was ready to take them home. The truck was parked in the shade under one of the hickory trees.

"Hi yawl this evening?" Mrs. Turpin asked grimly, appearing with the bucket and the dipper. There were three women and a boy in the truck.

"Us doin nicely," the oldest woman said. "Hi you doin?" and her gaze stuck immediately on the dark lump on Mrs. Turpin's forehead. "You done fell down, ain't you?" she asked in a solicitous voice. The old woman was dark and almost toothless. She had on an old felt hat of Claud's set back on her head. The other two women were younger and lighter and they both had new bright green sunhats. One of them had hers on her head; the other had taken hers off and the boy was grinning beneath it.

Mrs. Turpin set the bucket down on the floor of the truck. "Yawl hep yourselves," she said. She looked around to make sure Claud had gone. "No, I didn't fall down," she said, folding her arms. "It was something worse than that."

"Ain't nothing bad happen to you!" the old woman said. She said it as if they all knew that Mrs. Turpin was protected in some special way by Divine Providence. "You just had you a little fall."

"We were in town at the doctor's office for where the cow kicked Mr. Turpin," Mrs. Turpin said in a flat tone that indicated they could leave off their foolishness. "And there was this girl there. A big fat girl with her face all broke out. I could look at that girl and tell she was peculiar but I couldn't tell how. And me and her mama was just talking and going along and all of a sudden WHAM! She throws this big book she was reading at me and . . ."

"Naw!" the old woman cried out.

"And then she jumps over the table and commences to choke me."

"Naw!" they all exclaimed, "naw!"

"Hi come she do that?" the old woman asked. "What ail her?"

Mrs. Turpin only glared in front of her.

"Somethin ail her," the old woman said.

"They carried her off in an ambulance," Mrs. Turpin continued, "but before she went she was rolling on the floor and they were trying to hold her down to give her a shot and she said something to me." She paused. "You know what she said to me?"

"What she say?" they asked.

"She said," Mrs. Turpin began, and stopped, her face very dark and heavy. The sun was getting whiter and whiter, blanching the sky overhead so that the leaves of the hickory tree were black in the face of it. She could not bring forth the words. "Something real ugly," she muttered.

"She sho shouldn't said nothin ugly to you," the old woman said.

"You so sweet. You the sweetest lady I know."

"She pretty too," the one with the hat on said.

"And stout," the other one said. "I never knowed no sweeter white lady."

"That's the truth befo' Jesus," the old woman said. "Amen! You des as sweet and pretty as you can be."

Mrs. Turpin knew exactly how much Negro flattery was worth and it added to her rage. "She said," she began again and finished this time with a fierce rush of breath, "that I was an old wart hog from hell."

There was an astounded silence.

"Where she at?" the youngest woman cried in a piercing voice.

"Lemme see her. I'll kill her!"

"I'll kill her with you!" the other one cried.

"She b'long in the sylum," the old woman said emphatically.

"You the sweetest white lady I know."

"She pretty too," the other two said. "Stout as she can be and sweet. Jesus satisfied with her!"

"Deed he is," the old woman declared.

Idiots! Mrs. Turpin growled to herself. You could never say anything intelligent to a nigger. You could talk at them but not with them. "Yawl ain't drunk your water," she said shortly. "Leave the bucket in the truck when you're finished with it. I got more to do than just stand around and pass the time of day," and she moved off and into the house.

She stood for a moment in the middle of the kitchen. The dark protuberance over her eye looked like a miniature tornado cloud which might any moment sweep across the horizon of her brow. Her lower lip protruded dangerously. She squared her massive shoulders. Then she marched into the front of the house and out the side door and started down the road to the pig parlor. She had the look of a woman going single-handedly, weaponless, into battle.

The sun was a deep yellow now like a harvest moon and was riding westward very fast over the far tree line as if it meant to reach the hogs before she did. The road was rutted and she kicked several good-sized stones out of her path as she strode along. The pig parlor was on a little knoll at the end of a lane that ran off from the side of the barn. It was a square of concrete as large as a small room, with a board fence about four feet high around it. The concrete floor sloped slightly so that the hog wash could drain off into a trench where it was carried to the field for fertilizer. Claud was standing on the outside, on the edge of the concrete, hanging onto the top board, hosing down the floor inside. The hose was connected to the faucet of a water trough nearby.

Mrs. Turpin climbed up beside him and glowered down at the hogs inside. There were seven long-snouted bristly shoats in it—tan with liver-colored spots—and an old sow a few weeks off from farrowing. She was lying on her side grunting. The shoats were running about shaking themselves like idiot children, their little slit pig eyes searching the floor for anything left. She had read that pigs were the most intelligent animal. She doubted it. They were supposed to be smarter than dogs. There had even been a pig astronaut. He had performed his assignment perfectly but died of a heart attack afterwards because they left him in his electric suit, sitting upright throughout his examination when naturally a hog should be on all fours.

A-gruntin and a-rootin and a-groanin.

"Gimme that hose," she said, yanking it away from Claud. "Go on and carry them niggers home and then get off that leg."

"You look like you might have swallowed a mad dog," Claud observed, but he got down and limped off. He paid no attention to her humors.

Until he was out of earshot, Mrs. Turpin stood on the side of the pen, holding the hose and pointing the stream of water at the hind quarters of any shoat that looked as if it might try to lie down.

When he had had time to get over the hill, she turned her head slightly and her wrathful eyes scanned the path. He was nowhere in sight. She turned back again and seemed to gather herself up. Her shoulders rose and she drew in her breath.

"What do you send me a message like that for?" she said in a low fierce voice, barely above a whisper but with the force of a shout in its concentrated fury. "How am I a hog and me both? How am I saved and from hell too?" Her free fist was knotted and with the other she gripped the hose, blindly pointing the stream of water in and out of the eye of the old sow whose outraged squeal she did not hear.

The pig parlor commanded a view of the back pasture where their twenty beef cows were gathered around the hay-bales Claud and the boy had put out. The freshly cut pasture sloped down to the highway. Across it was their cotton field and beyond that a dark green dusty wood which they owned as well. The sun was behind the wood, very red, looking over the paling of trees like a farmer inspecting his own hogs.

"Why me?" she rumbled. "It's no trash around here, black or white, that I haven't given to. And break my back to the bone every day working. And do for the church."

She appeared to be the right size woman to command the arena before her. "How am I a hog?" she demanded. "Exactly how am I like them?" and she jabbed the stream of water at the shoats. "There was plenty of trash there. It didn't have to be me.

"If you like trash better, go get yourself some trash then," she railed. "You could have made me trash. Or a nigger. If trash is what you wanted, why didn't you make me trash?" She shook her fist with the hose in it and a watery snake appeared momentarily in the air. "I could quit working and take it easy and be filthy," she growled. "Lounge about the sidewalks all day drinking root beer. Dip snuff and spit in every puddle and have it all over my face. I could be nasty.

"Or you could have made me a nigger. It's too late for me to be a nigger," she said with deep sarcasm, "but I could act like one. Lay down in the middle of the road and stop traffic. Roll on the ground."

In the deepening light everything was taking on a mysterious hue. The pasture was growing a peculiar glassy green and the streak of highway had turned lavender. She braced herself for a final assault and this time her voice rolled out over the pasture. "Go on," she yelled, "call me a hog! Call me a hog again. From hell. Call me a wart hog from hell. Put that bottom rail on top. There'll still be a top and bottom!"

A garbled echo returned to her.

A final surge of fury shook her and she roared, "Who do you think you are?"

The color of everything, field and crimson sky, burned for a moment with a transparent intensity. The question carried over the pasture and across the highway and the cotton field and returned to her clearly like an answer from beyond the wood.

She opened her mouth but no sound came out of it.

A tiny truck, Claud's, appeared on the highway, heading rapidly out of sight. Its gears scraped thinly. It looked like a child's toy. At any moment a bigger truck might smash into it and scatter Claud's and the niggers' brains all over the road.

Mrs. Turpin stood there, her gaze fixed on the highway, all her muscles rigid, until in five or six minutes the truck reappeared, returning. She waited until it had had time to turn into their own road. Then like a monumental statue coming to life, she bent her head slowly and gazed, as if through the very heart of mystery, down into the pig parlor at the hogs. They had settled all in one corner around the old sow who was grunting softly. A red glow suffused them. They appeared to pant with a secret life.

Until the sun slipped finally behind the tree line, Mrs. Turpin remained there with her gaze bent to them as if she were absorbing some abysmal life-giving knowledge. At last she lifted her head. There was only a purple streak in the sky, cutting through a field of crimson and leading, like an extension of the highway, into the descending dusk. She raised her hands from the side of the pen in a gesture hieratic and profound. A visionary light settled in her eyes. She saw the streak as a vast swinging bridge extending upward from the earth through a field of living fire. Upon it a vast horde of souls were rumbling toward heaven. There were whole companies of white-trash, clean for the first time in their lives, and bands of black niggers in white robes, and battalions of freaks and lunatics shouting and clapping and leaping like frogs. And bringing up the end of the procession was a tribe of people whom she recognized at once as those who, like herself and Claud, had always had a little of everything and the God-given wit to use it right. She leaned forward to observe them closer. They were marching behind the others with great dignity, accountable as they had always been for good order and common sense and respectable behavior. They alone were on key. Yet she could see by their shocked and altered faces that even their virtues were being burned away. She lowered her hands and gripped the rail of the hog pen, her eyes small but fixed unblinkingly on what lay ahead. In a moment the vision faded but she remained where she was, immobile.

At length she got down and turned off the faucet and made her slow way on the darkening path to the house. In the woods around her the invisible cricket choruses had struck up, but what she heard were the voices of the souls climbing upward into the starry field and shouting hallelujah.

Guides to Reflection

1. During her college years at the Georgia College for Women, O'Connor did caricatures for the school newspaper. Something of the cartoonist's art

is apparent in her fiction: her eye for the telling detail, her ability to exaggerate and distort, her edge of satire. How is humor used in this story and to what purpose?

2. O'Connor uses the small group of people in the doctor's waiting room as a miniature social world that Mrs. Turpin is constantly sizing up. What impels her to make judgment after judgment? What is it about her that finally leads to her being judged, first by the accusation of Mary Grace ("Go back to hell where you came from, you old wart hog.") and then by the echo of her own words ("Who do you think you are?")?

3. Read Matthew 7:1-5. Do you see connections between this passage and the story? Explain.

4. When at the conclusion of "Revelation" Mrs. Turpin hears her own curse at God thrown back upon her, "She opened her mouth but no sound came out of it." In her unaccustomed silence she then sees two things: first, her husband's truck moving along the highway and steadily out of her sight, and then, secondly, a sow and her shoats in the pig parlor. From those two sights she then lifts her head and is filled with "visionary light." O'Connor doesn't spell out what she means here, but lets the reader do the work of interpretation. What do you make, on the one hand, of the truck on the highway and the pigs in their parlor, and, on the other, Mrs. Turpin's vision of souls "rumbling toward heaven"?

5. If grace is the power of God extended to human beings so that they may know something of God's nature and kingdom, how does grace function in this story? Who are its agents? How would you characterize what O'Connor spoke of as the "intrusions of grace" in this story? What does the girl Mary Grace have to do with it?

6. What did you "hear" as you listened for God in this story? What were your own revelations?

Frederick Buechner

For Frederick Buechner, theology and fiction are both essentially autobiographical, rooted in the human particulars that make up anyone's life story. But whereas the theologian typically leaves behind people, places, and events to create more abstract systems of thought, the fiction writer remains forever tied to the concrete. For poets and novelists, therefore, memory of the past is not simply the unspoken inspiration for talk about God, as it is for the systematic theologian; rather, it is the treasury from which the writer draws directly, the flesh and blood that refuses to be transformed into abstraction.

Or at least this is the way it has been for Buechner, a Presbyterian minister turned author, whose now almost thirty works are equally divided between fiction and nonfiction. As he confides in *The Alphabet of Grace*, "I cannot talk about God or sin or grace, for example, without at the same time talking about those parts of my own experience where these ideas became compelling and real."[1] In this same work Buechner renders a moment by moment account of a single day, hoping that readers will be able to see in the reconstruction of his personal world some reflection of their own existence. His purpose is to open up experience to the "holy and hidden heart of it," to keep track of the wonder we run away from or forget to notice. In particular, Buechner wants his readers to discover that all moments are key, that life itself is grounded in the mystery of God and shot through with divine grace. Each person's life story, therefore, is a scripture waiting to be read and interpreted, a sacred text capable of revealing nothing less than divine truth. All that is needed are eyes that see, ears that hear.

It has long been Buechner's vocation as a writer—of novels and essays, sermons and memoirs—to cultivate these capacities in his readers, to teach them to be theologians of autobiography. In doing so, he carries on the tradition inaugurated by St. Augustine's *Confessions* and carried on throughout the centuries. Like all "confessional" writers, Buechner offers his individual story as an example of how God works in any human life. From the perspective of faith he looks back on random experience and discovers pattern and purpose, a "figure in the carpet." Modesty prevents him from claiming some grand design unique to his experience, just as honesty keeps him from mending what remains broken or empty: not all the dots can be connected. But many can, and it is to this end that Buechner tells his story again and again, to share that vision of the gospel that theologian Paul Tillich first communicated to him in *The New Being*: "We want only to communicate to you an experience we have had that here and there in the world and now and then in ourselves is a New Creation, usually hidden, but sometimes manifest, and certainly manifest in Jesus who is called the Christ."[2] Here and there, now and then: this is where God is to be found—in ourselves.

Buechner traces his own discovery of God in a trio of memoirs written over the last decade: *The Sacred Journey* (1982), which tells of his boyhood, *Now and Then* (1983), with its account of his coming to maturity, and *Telling Secrets* (1991), which confides the struggles and insights of the last fifteen years. In addition to these forays into autobiography ("It is like telling somebody in detail how you are before they have asked the question, How are you?"[3]), Buechner has also occupied himself by writing novels about other men's lives. *Godric* (1980) and *Brendan* (1987) narrate the stories of two medieval saints, while *The Son of Laughter* (1993) tells the family history of Abraham and his seed from the perspective of Jacob. In each of these reconstructions of the past he returns to an age of faith when the longing for God and the desire to understand oneself as revealed in the divine mystery were more burning goals than they are today. None of these works, however, is nostalgic or antiquarian. Instead, each gives us an ancient figure who, though taken from a foreign world, is nonetheless our spiritual contemporary—as baffled as we are by the muddle of human life and as needful of religious meaning.

This need for meaning is explored in the chapter excerpted from *Telling Secrets* (1991). Buechner begins this most recent rendition of his life story by starting with his parents—the "charming, good-looking, gentle man" who took his own life when Buechner was only ten, the beautiful but distant woman whose heart was "rarely if ever touched in its deepest place." He looks back on them for a variety of reasons: to get even, to get on, or to say good-bye to the giants of childhood. But more deeply still, he attends to the mystery of his parents' lives because he knows that they live on in him—and that he in turn passes on their legacy to his own children.

At the painful heart of this chapter is Buechner's confrontation of his daughter's anorexia. He does not presume to tell her story; instead he tells his own, finding in his complex reactions to her refusal of food both his father's failure of courage and his mother's refusal to see or to hear. But after almost losing his life in an obsession with the fate of his daughter, he slowly learns the necessity of giving the girl her freedom and of taking up the burden of his own. In either case, he comes to emulate the "passionate restraint and hush" of a God who refuses to overpower, to save any of us from reality. Not knowing what disaster to expect as he enters his daughter's hospital room, he discovers instead the divine presence all around him: "God in his very stillness, holding his breath, loving her, loving us all, the only way he can without destroying us." As a result of his daughter's illness and recovery, he learns not only to trust that noncoercive love but, on a profoundly spiritual level, to mind his own business.

Having confided these very personal moments with the reader, Buechner then pulls back with the question that every autobiographer knows someone, somewhere, wants to ask: "Who cares?" His answers are complex: he tells his story so that readers will recognize in it something of their own; he writes so that we will all see that it is precisely in such stories as these that God is made known to each of us "most powerfully and personally." He shares his life, finally, in the conviction that the same God of history, who brought Israel out of Egypt and Christ out of the tomb, is even now working in the private histories of each and everyone of us. Therefore, just as we read the Bible in search of God's will, so should we attend to our own experience, aware that the Holy One is not a puppeteer pulling the strings, but a director helping us find ourselves in "the whole vast drama of things including our own small but crucial parts in it."

Buechner tells us that our lives are themselves sacred narratives, dramas, histories. Much of the past may be as painful as a father's suicide, a mother's withdrawal, a child's illness. But through the redeeming power of memory, "even the saddest things can become, once we have made peace with them, a source of wisdom and strength for the journey that still lies ahead."[4] To lose touch with one's own story is to run the risk of losing touch with God too. But to keep that story always in mind, says Buechner, is to remain open to the divine book that God is cowriting with each one of us—the book of our lives.

Peter S. Hawkins

Notes

1. Frederick Buechner, *The Alphabet of Grace* (New York: Seabury, 1970), 4.
2. Paul Tillilch, *The New Being* (New York: Scribners, 1955), 18.
3. Frederick Buechner, *Telling Secrets* (New York: HarperCollins Publishers, 1991), 1.

The Dwarves in the Stable

One November morning in 1936 when I was ten years old, my father got up early, put on a pair of gray slacks and a maroon sweater, opened the door to look in briefly on my younger brother and me, who were playing a game in our room, and then went down into the garage where he turned on the engine of the family Chevy and sat down on the running board to wait for the exhaust to kill him. Except for a memorial service for his Princeton class the next spring, by which time we had moved away to another part of the world altogether, there was no funeral because on both my mother's side and my father's there was no church connection of any kind and funerals were simply not part of the tradition. He was cremated, his ashes buried in a cemetery in Brooklyn, and I have no idea who if anybody was present. I know only that my mother, brother, and I were not.

There was no funeral to mark his death and put a period at the end of the sentence that had been his life, and as far as I can remember, once he had died my mother, brother, and I rarely talked about him much ever again, either to each other or to anybody else. It made my mother too sad to talk about him, and since there was already more than enough sadness to go round, my brother and I avoided the subject with her as she avoided it for her own reasons also with us. Once in a while she would bring it up but only in very oblique ways. I remember her saying things like "You're going to have to be big boys now" and "Now things are going to be different for all of us," and to me, "You're the man of the family now," with that one little three-letter adverb freighted with more grief and anger and guilt and God knows what all else than it could possibly bear.

We didn't talk about my father with each other, and we didn't talk about him outside the family either partly at least because suicide was looked on as something a little shabby and shameful in those days. Nice people weren't supposed to get mixed up with it. My father had tried to keep it a secret himself by leaving his note to my mother in a place where only she would be likely to find it and by saying a number of times the last few weeks of his life that there was something wrong with the Chevy's exhaust system, which he was going to see if he could fix. He did this partly in hopes that his life insurance wouldn't be invalidated, which of course it was, and partly too, I guess, in hopes that his friends wouldn't find out how he had died, which of course they did. His suicide was a secret we nonetheless tried to keep as best we could, and after a while my father himself became such a secret. There were times when he almost seemed a secret we were trying to keep from each other. I suppose there were occasions when one of us said, "Remember the time he did this," or, "Remember the time he said that," but if so, I've long since forgotten them. And because words are so much a part of what we keep the past alive by, if only words to ourselves, by not speaking of what we remembered about him we soon simply stopped remembering at all, or at least I did.

Within a couple of months of his death we moved away from New Jersey, where he had died, to the island of Bermuda of all places—another house, another country even—and from that point on I can't even remember remembering him. Within a year of his death I seem to have forgotten what he looked like except for certain photographs of him, to have forgotten what his voice sounded like and what it had been like to be with him. Because none of the three of us ever talked about how we had felt about him when he was alive or how we felt about him now that he wasn't, those feelings soon disappeared too and went underground along with the memories. As nearly as I can find out from people who knew him, he was a charming, good-looking, gentle man who was down on his luck and drank too much and had a great number of people who loved him and felt sorry for him. Among those people, however inadequately they may have showed it, I can only suppose were his wife and two sons; but in almost no time at all, it was as if, at least for me, he had never existed.

Don't talk, don't trust, don't feel is supposed to be the unwritten law of families that for one reason or another have gone out of whack, and certainly it was our law. We never talked about what had happened. We didn't trust the world with our secret, hardly even trusted each other with it. And as far as my ten-year-old self was concerned anyway, the only feeling I can remember from that distant time was the blessed relief of coming out of the dark and unmentionable sadness of my father's life and death into fragrance and greenness and light.

Don't talk, trust, feel was the law we lived by, and woe to the one who broke it. Twenty-two years later in a novel called *The Return of Ansel Gibbs* I told a very brief and fictionalized version of my father's death, and the most accurate word I can find to describe my mother's reaction to it is fury. For days she could hardly bring herself to speak to me, and when she did, it was with words of great bitterness. As she saw it, I had betrayed a sacred trust, and though I might have defended myself by saying that the story was after all as much mine as his son to tell as it was hers as his widow to keep hidden, I not only didn't say any such things but never even considered such things. I felt as much of a traitor as she charged me with being, and at the age of thirty-two was as horrified at what I had done as if I had been a child of ten. I was full of guilt and remorse and sure that in who-knows-what grim and lasting way I would be made to suffer for what I had done.

I was in my fifties and my mother in her eighties before I dared write on the forbidden subject again. It was in an autobiographical book called *The Sacred Journey* that I did so, and this time I told the story straight except that out of deference to her, or perhaps out of fear of her, I made no reference to her part in it. Otherwise I set it down as fully and accurately as I could, and the only reason I was able to do so was that I suspected that from *Ansel Gibbs* on my mother had never really read any other book I had written for fear of what she might find there. I was sure that she wouldn't read this one, either. And I turned out to be right. She never read the book or the second autobiographical one that followed it even though, or precisely because, it was the story of her son's life and in that sense a part of her own story too. She was a strong and brave woman in many ways, but she was not brave and strong enough for that. We all have to survive as best we can.

She survived to within eleven days of her ninety-second birthday and died in her own bed in the room that for the last year or so of her life when her arthritic knees made it virtually impossible for her to walk became the only world that really interested her. She kept track more or less of the world outside. She had a rough idea what her children and grandchildren were up to. She read the papers and watched the evening news. But such things as that were dim and far away compared to the news that was breaking around her every day. Yvonne, who came days, had been trying to tell her something but God only knew what, her accent was so thick. Marge, who came nights, was an hour late because of delays on the subway, or so she said. My mother's cane had fallen behind the radiator, and the super was going to have to come do something about it. Where was her fan? Where was the gold purse she kept her extra hearing aids in? Where was the little peach-colored pillow, which of all the pillows she had was the only one that kept her tray level when they brought in her meals? In the world where she lived, these were the things that made headlines.

"If I didn't have something to look for, I would be lost," she said once. It was one of her most shimmering utterances. She hunted for her lost pills, lost handkerchief, lost silver comb, the little copy of *Les Malheurs de Sophie* she had lost, because with luck she might even find them. There was a better chance of it anyway than of finding her lost beauty or the friends who had mostly died or the life that had somehow gotten mislaid in the debris of her nonlife, all the aches and pains and indignities of having outlived almost everything including herself. But almost to the end she could laugh till the tears ran down and till our tears ran down. She loved telling how her father in the confusion of catching a train handed the red-cap his wallet once, or how one of her beaux had stepped through somebody's straw hat in the hall closet and was afraid to come out. Her laughter came from deep down in herself and deep down in the past, which in one way was lost and gone and in other ways was still as much within her reach as the can of root beer with a straw sticking in it which she always had on her bedside table because she said it was the only thing that helped her dry throat. The sad times she kept locked away never to be named, but the funny, happy times, the glamorous, romantic, young times, continued to be no less a part of her life than the furniture.

She excoriated the ravages of old age but never accepted them as the inevitable consequence of getting old. "I don't know what's wrong with me today," she must have said a thousand days as she tried once, then again, then a third time, to pull herself out of her chair into her walker. It never seemed to occur to her that what was wrong with her was that she was on her way to pushing a hundred. Maybe that was why some part of her remained unravaged. Some surviving lightness of touch let her stand back from the wreckage and see that among other things it was absurdly funny. When I told her the last time she was mobile enough to visit us in Vermont that the man who had just passed her window was the gardener, she said, "Tell him to come in and take a look at the last rose of summer."

She liked to paste gold stars on things or to antique things with gold paint—it was what she did with the past too of course—and lampshades, chairs, picture frames, tables, gleamed like treasure in the crazy little museum of her bedroom. The chaise lounge was heaped with pillows, a fake leopard-skin throw, a velvet quilt, fashion magazines, movie magazines, catalogues stacked on a table beside it, stories by Dorothy Parker and Noel Coward, Kahlil Gibran's *The Prophet*. Victorian beadwork pincushions hung from the peach-colored walls along with pictures of happier times, greener places. The closet was a cotillion of pretty clothes she hadn't been able to wear for years, and her bureau overflowed with more of them—blouses, belts, costume jewelry, old evening purses, chiffon scarves, gloves. On top of the bureau stood perfume bottles, pill bottles, jars, tubes, boxes of patent medicine, a bowl of M & Ms, which she said were good for her. She had a theory that when you had a craving for something, including M & Ms, it means that your system needs it.

The living heart and command center of that room was the dressing table. When she was past getting out of her bed to sit at it any longer, what she needed from it was brought to her on a tray as soon as she woke up every morning, before breakfast even—the magnifying mirror, the lipsticks, eyebrow pencils, tweezers, face powder, hair brush, combs, cold cream, mascara. Before she did anything else, she did that and did it with such artistry that even within weeks of her end she managed a not implausible version of the face that since girlhood had been her principal fame and fairest fortune.

Over that dressing table there hung for years a mirror that I can remember from childhood. It was a mirror with an olive green wooden frame which she had once painted in oils with a little garland of flowers and medallions bearing the French words: *Il faut souffrir pour être belle.* It was the motto of her life: You have to suffer in order to be beautiful. What she meant, of course, was all the pains she took in front of the mirror: the plucking and primping and powdering, the brushing and painting—that kind of suffering. But it seems clear that there was another kind too. To be born as blonde and blue-eyed and beautiful as she was can be as much of a handicap in its way as to be born with a cleft palate because if you are beautiful enough you don't really have to be anything much else to make people love you and want to be near you. You don't have to be particularly kind or unselfish or generous or compassionate because people will flock around you anyway simply for the sake of your *beaux yeux*. My mother could be all of those good things when she took a notion to, but she never made a habit of it. She never developed the giving, loving side of what she might have been as a human being, and, needless to say, that was where the real suffering came—the two failed marriages after the death of my father, the fact that among all the friends she had over the course of her life, she never as far as I know had one whom she would in any sense have sacrificed herself for and by doing so might perhaps have begun to find her best and truest self. W. B. Yeats in his poem "A Prayer for My Daughter" writes, "Hearts are not had as a gift but hearts are earned/By those that are not entirely beautiful." My almost entirely beautiful mother was by no means heartless, but I think hers was a heart that, who knows why, was rarely if ever touched in its deepest place. To let it be touched there was a risk that for reasons known only to her she was apparently not prepared to take.

For the twenty years or so she lived in New York she made no new friends because she chose to make none and lost all contact with the few old ones who were still alive. She believed in God, I think. With her eyes shut she would ask me what I thought about the afterlife from time to time, though when I tried to tell her she of course couldn't hear because it is hard to shout anything very much about the afterlife. But she never went to church. It always made her cry, she said. She wouldn't have been caught dead joining a club or group of any kind. "I know I'm queer," she often said. "I'm a very private person." And it was true. Even with the people closest to her she rarely spoke of what was going on inside her skin or asked that question of them. For the last fifteen years or so it reached the point where she saw virtually nobody except her immediate family and most of them not often. But by a miracle it didn't destroy her.

She had a cruel and terrible tongue when she was angry. When she struck, she struck to kill, and such killings must have been part of what she closed her eyes to, together with the other failures and mistakes of her life and the guilt they caused her, the shame she felt. But she never became bitter. She turned away from the world but never turned in upon herself. It was a kind of miracle, really. If she was lonely, I never heard her complain about it. Instead it was her looks she complained about: *My hair looks like straw. When I wake up in the morning I have this awful red spot on my cheek. These God-awful teeth don't fit. I don't know what's wrong with me today.* From somewhere she was nourished, in other words, and richly nourished, God only knows how, God only knows. That was the other part of the miracle. Something deep within her stayed young, stayed beautiful even, was never lost. And till the end of her life she was as successful at not facing the reality of being a very old woman as for almost a century she was successful at not facing her dark times as a young one.

Being beautiful was her business, her art, her delight, and it took her a long way and earned her many dividends, but when, as she saw it, she lost her beauty—you stand a better chance of finding your cane behind the radiator than ever finding blue eyes and golden hair again—she was like a millionaire who runs out of money. She took her name out of the phone book and got an unlisted number. She eventually became so deaf that it became almost impossible to speak to her except about things simple enough to shout—her health, the weather, when you would be seeing her next. It was as if deafness was a technique she mastered for not hearing anything that might threaten her peace. She developed the habit of closing her eyes when she spoke to you as if you were a dream she was dreaming. It was as if she chose not to see in your face what you might be thinking behind the simple words you were shouting, or as if, ostrich-like, closing her eyes was a way of keeping you from seeing her. With her looks gone she felt she had nothing left to offer the world, to propitiate the world. So what she did was simply to check out of the world—that old, last rose of summer—the way Greta Garbo and Marlene Dietrich checked out of it, holing themselves up somewhere and never venturing forth except in disguise. My mother holed herself up in her apartment on 79th Street, then in just one room of that apartment, then in just one chair in that room, and finally in the bed where one morning a few summers ago, perhaps in her sleep, she died at last.

It is so easy to sum up other people's lives like this, and necessary too, of course, especially our parents' lives. It is a way of reducing their giant figures to a size we can manage, I suppose, a way of getting even maybe, of getting on, of saying goodbye. The day will come when somebody tries to sum you up the same way and also me. Tell me about old Buechner then. What was he really like? What made him tick? How did his story go? Well, you see, this happened and then that happened, and then that, and that is why he became thus and so, and why when all is said and done it is not so hard to understand why things turned out for him as they finally did. Is there any truth at all in the patterns we think we see, the explanations and insights that fall so readily from our tongues? Who knows. The main thing that leads me to believe that what I've said about my mother has at least a kind of partial truth is that I know at first hand that it is true of the mother who lives on in me and will always be part of who I am.

In the mid 1970s, as a father of three teenage children and a husband of some twenty years standing by then, I would have said that my hearing was pretty good, that I could hear not only what my wife and children were saying but lots of things they weren't saying too. I would have said that I saw fairly well what was going on inside our house and what was going on inside me. I would also have said if anybody had asked me that our family was a close and happy one—that we had our troubles like everybody else but that we loved each other and respected each other and understood each other better than most. And in a hundred ways, praise God, I believe I was right. I believe that is the way it was. But in certain other ways, I came to learn, I was as deaf as my mother was with her little gold purse full of hearing aids none of which really ever worked very well, and though I did not shut my eyes when I talked to people the way she did, I shut them without knowing it to a whole dimension of the life that my wife and I and our children were living together on a green hillside in Vermont during those years.

There are two pieces of stained glass that sit propped up in one of the windows in the room where I write—a room paneled in old barn siding gone silvery gray with maybe as much as two centuries of weathering and full of a great many books, many of them considerably older than that which I've collected over the years and try to keep oiled and repaired because books are my passion, not only writing them and every once in a while even reading them but just having them and moving them around and feeling the comfort of their serene presence. One of those pieces of stained glass, which I think I asked somebody to give me one Christmas, shows the Cowardly Lion from *The Wizard of Oz* with his feet bound with rope and his face streaming with tears as a few of the Winged Monkeys who have bound him hover around in the background. The other is a diptych that somebody gave me once and that always causes me a twinge of embarrassment when I notice it because it seems a little too complacently religious. On one of its panels are written the words "May the blessing of God crown this house" and on the other "Fortunate is he whose work is blessed and whose household is prospered by the Lord."

I have never given either the lion or the diptych much thought as they've sat there year after year gathering dust, but I happened to notice them as I was preparing these pages and decided they might well serve as a kind of epigraph for this part of the story I'm telling. The Cowardly Lion is me, of course—crying, tied up, afraid. I am crying because at the time I'm speaking of, some fifteen years ago, a lot of sad and scary things were going on in our house that I felt helpless either to understand or to do anything about. Yet despite its rather self-satisfied religiosity, I believe the diptych is telling a truth about that time too.

I believe the blessing of God was indeed crowning our house in the sense that the sad and scary things themselves were, as it turned out, a fearsome blessing. And all the time those things were happening, the very fact that I was able to save my sanity by continuing to write among other things a novel called *Godric* made my work blessed and a means of grace at least for me. Nothing I've ever written came out of a darker time or brought me more light and comfort. It also—far more than I realized at the time I wrote it—brought me a sharper glimpse than I had ever had before of the crucial role my father has always played in my life and continues to play in my life even though in so many ways I have long since lost all but a handful of conscious memories of him.

I did not realize until after I wrote it how much of this there is in the book. When Godric is about to leave home to make his way in the world and his father Aedlward raises his hand to him in farewell, Godric says, "I believe my way went from that hand as a path goes from a door, and though many a mile that way has led me since, with many a turn and crossroad in between, if ever I should trace it back, it's to my father's hand that it would lead." And later, when he learns of his father's death, he says, "The sadness was I'd lost a father I had never fully found. It's like a tune that ends before you've heard it out. Your whole life through you search to catch the strain, and seek the face you've lost in strangers' faces." In writing passages like that, I was writing more than I had known I knew with the result that the book was not only a word *from me*—my words painstakingly chosen and arranged into sentences by me alone—but also a word out of such a deep and secret part of who I am that it seemed also a word to me.

If writers write not just with paper and ink or a word processor but with their own life's blood, then I think something like this is perhaps always the case. A book you write out of the depths of who you are, like a dream you dream out of those same depths, is entirely your own creation. All the words your characters speak are words that you alone have put into their mouths, just as every situation they become involved in is one that you alone have concocted for them. But it seems to me nonetheless that a book you write, like a dream you dream, can have more healing and truth and wisdom in it at least for yourself than you feel in any way responsible for.

A large part of the truth that Godric had for me was the truth that although death ended my father, it has never ended my relationship with my father—a secret that I had never so clearly understood before. So forty-four years after the last time I saw him, it was to my father that I dedicated the book—*In memoriam patris mei*. I wrote the dedication in Latin solely because at the time it seemed appropriate to the medieval nature of the tale, but I have come to suspect since that Latin was also my unconscious way of remaining obedient to the ancient family law that the secret of my father must be at all costs kept secret.

The other half of the diptych's message—"whose household is prospered by the Lord"—was full of irony. Whether because of the Lord or good luck or the state of the stock market, we were a prosperous family in more ways than just economic, but for all the good our prosperity did us when the chips were down, we might as well have been paupers.

What happened was that one of our daughters began to stop eating. There was nothing scary about it at first. It was just the sort of thing any girl who thought she'd be prettier if she lost a few pounds might do—nothing for breakfast, maybe a carrot or a Diet Coke for lunch, for supper perhaps a little salad with low calorie dressing. But then, as months went by, it did become scary. Anorexia nervosa is the name of the sickness she was suffering from, needless to say, and the best understanding of it that I have been able to arrive at goes something like this. Young people crave to be free and independent. They crave also to be taken care of and safe. The dark magic of anorexia is that it satisfies both of these cravings at once. By not eating, you take your stand against the world that is telling you what to do and who to be. And by not eating you also make your body so much smaller, lighter, weaker that in effect it becomes a child's body again and the world flocks to your rescue. This double victory is so great that apparently not even self-destruction seems too high a price to pay.

Be that as it may, she got more and more thin, of course, till she began to have the skull-like face and fleshless arms and legs of a victim of Buchenwald, and at the same time the Cowardly Lion got more and more afraid and sad, felt more and more helpless. No rational argument, no dire medical warning, no pleading or cajolery or bribery would make this young woman he loved eat normally again but only seemed to strengthen her determination not to, this young woman on whose life his own in so many ways depended. He could not solve her problem because he was of course himself part of her problem. She remained very much the same person she had always been—creative, loving, funny, bright as a star—but she was more afraid of gaining weight than she was afraid of death itself because that was what it came to finally. Three years were about as long as the sickness lasted in its most intense form with some moments when it looked as though things were getting better and some moments when it was hard to imagine they could get any worse. Then finally, when she had to be hospitalized, a doctor called one morning to say that unless they started feeding her against her will, she would die. It was as clear-cut as that. Tears ran down the Cowardly Lion's face as he stood with the telephone at his ear. His paws were tied. The bat-winged monkeys hovered.

I will not try to tell my daughter's story for two reasons. One is that it is not mine to tell but hers. The other is that of course I do not know her story, not the real story, the inside story, of what it was like for her. For the same reasons I will not try to tell what it was like for my wife or our other two children, each of whom in her own way was involved in that story. I can tell only my part in it, what happened to me, and even there I can't be sure I have it right because in many ways it is happening still. The fearsome blessing of that hard time continues to work itself out in my life in the same way we're told the universe is still hurtling through outer space under the impact of the great cosmic explosion that brought it into being in the first place. I think grace sometimes explodes into our lives like that—sending our pain, terror, astonishment hurtling through inner space until by grace they become Orion, Cassiopeia, Polaris to give us our bearings, to bring us into something like full being at last.

My anorectic daughter was in danger of starving to death, and without knowing it, so was I. I wasn't living my own life any more because I was so caught up in hers. If in refusing to eat she was mad as a hatter, I was if anything madder still because whereas in some sense she knew what she was doing to herself, I knew nothing at all about what I was doing to myself. She had given up food. I had virtually given up doing anything in the way of feeding myself humanly. To be at peace is to have peace inside yourself more or less in spite of what is going on outside yourself. In that sense I had no peace at all. If on one particular day she took it into her head to have a slice of toast, say, with her dietetic supper, I was in seventh heaven. If on some other day she decided to have no supper at all, I was in hell.

I choose the term *hell* with some care. Hell is where there is no light but only darkness, and I was so caught up in my fear for her life, which had become in a way my life too, that none of the usual sources of light worked any more, and light was what I was starving for. I had the companionship of my wife and two other children. I read books. I played tennis and walked in the woods. I saw friends and went to the movies. But even in the midst of such times as that I remained so locked inside myself that I was not really present in them at all. Toward the end of C. S. Lewis's *The Last Battle* there is a scene where a group of dwarves sit huddled together in a tight little knot thinking that they are in a pitch black, malodorous stable when the truth of it is that they are out in the midst of an endless grassy countryside as green as Vermont with the sun shining and blue sky overhead. The huge golden lion, Aslan himself, stands nearby with all the other dwarves "kneeling in a circle around his forepaws" as Lewis writes, "and burying their hands and faces in his mane as he stooped his great head to touch them with his tongue." When Aslan offers the dwarves food, they think it is offal. When he offers them wine, they take it for ditch water. "Perfect love casteth out fear," John writes (1 John 4:18), and the other side of that is that fear like mine casteth out love, even God's love. The love I had for my daughter was lost in the anxiety I had for my daughter.

The only way I knew to be a father was to take care of her, as my father had been unable to take care of me, to move heaven and earth if necessary to make her well, and of course I couldn't do that. I didn't have either the wisdom or the power to make her well. None of us has the power to change other human beings like that, and it would be a terrible power if we did, the power to violate the humanity of others even for their own good. The psychiatrists we consulted told me I couldn't cure her. The best thing I could do for her was to stop trying to do anything. I think in heart I knew they were right, but it didn't stop the madness of my desperate meddling, it didn't stop the madness of my trying. Everything I could think to do or say only stiffened her resolve to be free from, among other things, me.

Her not eating was a symbolic way of striking out for that freedom. The only way she would ever be well again was if and when she freely chose to be. The best I could do as her father was to stand back and give her that freedom even at the risk of her using it to choose for death instead of life.

Love your neighbor as yourself is part of the great commandment. The other way to say it is, Love yourself as your neighbor. Love yourself not in some egocentric, self-serving sense but love yourself the way you would love your friend in the sense of taking care of yourself, nourishing yourself, trying to understand, comfort, strengthen yourself. Ministers in particular, people in the caring professions in general, are famous for neglecting their selves with the result that they are apt to become in their own way as helpless and crippled as the people they are trying to care for and thus no longer selves who can be of much use to anybody. If your daughter is struggling for life in a raging torrent, you do not save her by jumping into the torrent with her, which leads only to your both drowning together. Instead you keep your feet on the dry bank—you maintain as best you can your own inner peace, the best and strongest of who you are—and from that solid ground reach out a rescuing hand. "Mind your own business" means butt out of other people's lives because in the long run they must live their lives for themselves, but it also means pay mind to your own life, your own health and wholeness, both for your own sake and ultimately for the sake of those you love too. Take care of yourself so you can take care of them. A bleeding heart is of no help to anybody if it bleeds to death.

How easy it is to write such words and how impossible it was to live them. What saved the day for my daughter was that when she finally had to be hospitalized in order to keep her alive, it happened about three thousand miles away from me. I was not there to protect her, to make her decisions, to manipulate events on her behalf, and the result was that she had to face those events on her own. There was no one to shield her from those events and their consequences in all their inexorability. In the form of doctors, nurses, social workers, the judge who determined that she was a danger to her own life and thus could be legally hospitalized against her will, society stepped in. Those men and women were not haggard, dithering, lovesick as I was. They were realistic, tough, conscientious, and in those ways, though they would never have put it in such terms themselves, loved her in a sense that I believe is closer to what Jesus meant by love than what I had been doing.

God loves in something like their way, I think. The power that created the universe and spun the dragonfly's wing and is beyond all other powers holds back, in love, from overpowering us. I have never felt God's presence more strongly than when my wife and I visited that distant hospital where our daughter was. Walking down the corridor to the room that had her name taped to the door, I felt that presence surrounding me like air—God in his very stillness, holding his breath, loving her, loving us all, the only way he can without destroying us. One night we went to compline in an Episcopal cathedral, and in the coolness and near emptiness of that great vaulted place, in the remoteness of the choir's voices chanting plainsong, in the grayness of the stone, I felt it again—the passionate restraint and hush of God.

Little by little the young woman I loved began to get well, emerging out of the shadows finally as strong and sane and wise as anybody I know, and little by little as I watched her healing happen, I began to see how much I was in need of healing and getting well myself. Like Lewis's dwarves, for a long time I had sat huddled in the dark of a stable of my own making. It was only now that I started to suspect the presence of the green countryside, the golden lion in whose image and likeness even cowardly lions are made.

This is all part of the story about what it has been like for the last ten years or so to be me, and before anybody else has the chance to ask it, I will ask it myself: Who cares? What in the world could be less important than who I am and who my father and mother were, the mistakes I have made together with the occasional discoveries, the bad times and good times, the moments of grace. If I were a public figure and my story had had some impact on the world at large, that might be some justification for telling it, but I am a very private figure indeed, living very much out of the mainstream of things in the hills of Vermont, and my life has had very little impact on anybody much except for the people closest to me and the comparative few who have read books I've written and been one way or another touched by them.

But I talk about my life anyway because if, on the one hand, hardly anything could be less important, on the other hand, hardly anything could be more important. My story is important not because it is mine, God knows, but because if I tell it anything like right, the chances are you will recognize that in many ways it is also yours. Maybe nothing is more important than that we keep track, you and I, of these stories of who we are and where we have come from and the people we have met along the way because it is precisely through these stories in all their particularity, as I have long believed and often said, that God makes himself known to each of us most powerfully and personally. If this is true, it means that to lose track of our stories is to be profoundly impoverished not only humanly but also spiritually.

The God of biblical faith is a God who started history going in the first place. He is also a God who moment by moment, day by day continues to act in history always, which means both the history that gets written down in the *New York Times* and the *San Francisco Chronicle* and at the same time my history and your history, which for the most part don't get written down anywhere except in the few lines that may be allotted to us some day on the obituary page. The Exodus, the Covenant, the entry into the Promised Land—such mighty acts of God as these appear in Scripture, but no less mighty are the acts of God as they appear in our own lives. I think of my father's death as in its way his exodus, his escape from bondage, and of the covenant that my mother made with my brother and me never to talk about him, and of the promised land of pre-World War II Bermuda that we reached through the wilderness and bewilderness of our first shock and grief at losing him.

As I understand it, to say that God is mightily present even in such private events as these does not mean that he makes events happen to us which move us in certain directions like chessmen. Instead, events happen under their own steam as random as rain, which means that God is present in them not as their cause but as the one who even in the hardest and most hair-raising of them offers us the possibility of that new life and healing which I believe is what salvation is. For instance I cannot believe that a God of love and mercy in any sense willed my father's suicide; it was only father himself who willed it as the only way out available to him from a life that for various reasons he had come to find unbearable. God did not will what happened that early November morning in Essex Falls, New Jersey, but I believe that God was present in what happened. I cannot guess how he was present with my father—I can guess much better how utterly abandoned by God my father must have felt if he thought about God at all—but my faith as well as my prayer is that he was and continues to be present with him in ways beyond my guessing. I can speak with some assurance only of how God was present in that dark time for me in the sense that I was not destroyed by it but came out of it with scars that I bear to this day, to be sure, but also somehow the wiser and the stronger for it. Who knows how I might have turned out if my father had lived, but through the loss of him all those long years ago I think that I learned something about how even tragedy can be a means of grace that I might never have come to any other way. As I see it, in other words, God acts in history and in your and my brief histories not as the puppeteer who sets the scene and works the strings but rather as the great director who no matter what role fate casts us in conveys to us somehow from the wings, if we have our eyes, ears, hearts open and sometimes even if we don't, how we can play those roles in a way to enrich and ennoble and hallow the whole vast drama of things including our own small but crucial parts in it.

In fact I am inclined to believe that God's chief purpose in giving us memory is to enable us to go back in time so that if we didn't play those roles right the first time round, we can still have another go at it now. We cannot undo our old mistakes or their consequences any more than we can erase old wounds that we have both suffered and inflicted, but through the power that memory gives us of thinking, feeling, imagining our way back through time we can at long last finally finish with the past in the sense of removing its power to hurt us and other people and to stunt our growth as human beings.

The sad things that happened long ago will always remain part of who we are just as the glad and gracious things will too, but instead of being a burden of guilt, recrimination, and regret that make us constantly stumble as we go, even the saddest things can become, once we have made peace with them, a source of wisdom and strength for the journey that still lies ahead. It is through memory that we are able to reclaim much of our lives that we have long since written off by finding that in everything that has happened to us over the years God was offering us possibilities of new life and healing which, though we may have missed them at the time, we can still choose and be brought to life by and healed by all these years later.

Another way of saying it, perhaps, is that memory makes it possible for us both to bless the past, even those parts of it that we have always felt cursed by, and also to be blessed by it. If this kind of remembering sounds like what psychotherapy is all about, it is because of course it is, but I think it is also what the forgiveness of sins is all about—the interplay of God's forgiveness of us and our forgiveness of God and each other. To see how God's mercy was for me buried deep even in my father's death was not just to be able to forgive my father for dying and God for letting him die so young and without hope and all the people like my mother who were involved in his death but also to be able to forgive myself for all the years I had failed to air my crippling secret so that then, however slowly and uncertainly, I could start to find healing. It is in the experience of such healing that I believe we experience also God's loving forgiveness of us, and insofar as memory is the doorway to both experiences, it becomes not just therapeutic but sacred.

In a book called *The Wizard's Tide* I wrote the story of my father's death the way I would tell it to a child, in other words the way I need to tell it to the child who lives on inside me as the children we were live on inside all of us. By telling it as a story, I told it not from the outside as an observer, the way I have told it in these pages, but from the inside as a participant. By telling it in language a child could understand, I told it as the child who I both was in 1936 and still am in 1990. I relived it for that child and as that child with the difference that this time I was able to live it right.

The father in the story dies in much the way my father did, and the mother and the children in the story hushed it up in much the way my mother and her two children did, but there comes the difference. At the end of the story, on Christmas eve, the boy Teddy, who is me, comes to a momentous conclusion. "He thought about how terrible it was that nobody talked about [his father] any more so that it was almost as if there had never been any such person. He decided that from now on he wanted to talk about him a lot. He wanted to remember everything about him that he could remember so someday he could tell about him to other people who had never seen him." And then, just before turning off the lights, Teddy actually does this. For the first time since his father's death, Teddy brings the subject up to his younger sister, Bean. He doesn't say anything about his father, he just mentions his name, but as I wrote the story, I knew that was enough. It was enough to start a healing process for the children in the story that for me didn't start till I was well into my fifties. Stranger still, it was enough also to start healing the child in me the way he might have been healed in 1936 if his real story had only turned out like the make-believe story in the book. By a kind of miracle, the make-believe story *became* the real story or vice versa. The unalterable past was in some extraordinary way altered. Maybe the most sacred function of memory is just that: to render the distinction between past, present, and future ultimately meaningless; to enable us at some level of our being to inhabit that same eternity which it is said that God himself inhabits. . . .*

Guides to Reflection

1. Buechner uses two objects in his study as aids to memory. One is a piece of stained glass that shows the Cowardly Lion from *The Wizard of Oz*; the other is a paneled plaque that on one side reads, "May the blessing of God crown this house," and on the other, "Fortunate is he whose work is blessed and whose household is prospered by the Lord." Both the piece

---

*The conclusion of "The Dwarves in the Stable" has been omitted with permission of the publisher.

of glass and the diptych panel recall him to himself and to the paradoxes of his life. Explore how each of these objects serves him as a key to open the past and to recollect himself. Do any such objects function in this way for you? If so, what are they and what do they recall or reveal?

2. One of the powerful aspects of Buechner's writing is its candor, especially when it comes to evaluating the impact of close family members. In the case of his father, mother, and daughter, he attempts to understand the roles they have played not only in his experience but in his religious life. Are you able to describe your own close relationships in this way? Explain your answer if you can.

3. Buechner challenges us to take our own experience as seriously as we do the events of Scripture. He refers to the mighty acts of God made manifest in his own life and indeed sees them as analogues to biblical story: "I think of my father's death as in its way his exodus, his escape from bondage, and of the covenant my mother made with my brother and me never to talk about him. . . ." To what degree do you find this appropriation of the Bible valid and useful for understanding the events of your own life? How is your personal history "biblical"?

4. The wisdom Buechner gains from his daughter's struggle with anorexia is prayerfully and lovingly to mind his own business. Part of the problem in the family situation, as he comes to see it, is his overinvolvement with his daughter; he must learn to let her alone, to pay attention to himself. What do you make of this analysis? How do you react to Buechner's statement, "The best I could do as her father was to stand back and give her that freedom even at the risk of her using it to choose death instead of life"?

5. Buechner writes, "memory makes it possible for us both to bless the past, even those parts we have always felt cursed by, and also to be blessed by it." Has this been true for you? If so, how?

Patricia Hampl

In her book *Virgin Time*,[1] Patricia Hampl describes a conversation about religion she had as a young girl with her eccentric next door neighbor Mr. Bertram:

> No, he said, he did not go to church. "But you do believe in God?" I asked, hardly daring to hope he did not. He paused for a moment and looked up at the sky, where big, spreading clouds streamed by. "God isn't the problem," he said.
>
> Some ancient fissure split open, a fine crack in reality: so there *was* a problem. Just as I'd always felt.... (p. 62)

Virgin Time, whose subtitle is *A Search for the Contemplative Life*, tells the stories of three pilgrimages Hampl takes in pursuit of that "problem." She seeks to define it, tries to frame an appropriate response to it, and observes other people's struggles with it.

The author of two collections of poetry and two autobiographical books, Hampl comes to the religious issues in *Virgin Time* after having addressed significant cultural ones in her earlier work. In the memoir *A Romantic Education*, for instance, Hampl tells the story of her attempt to establish a connection with the Czech culture that her immigrant grandparents left behind when they came to the United States. She describes two journeys to Prague and her efforts on them to satisfy her longing for the past. *Virgin Time* is also a book about journeys, but it describes a different kind of journey, the pilgrimage. On pilgrimage, people travel specific, mapped routes along which certain places hold spiritual significance. At each of these places, the pilgrim hopes to do one of a number of things: praise God, learn something, be healed, have a vision.

Hampl's role on her three pilgrimages is primarily that of an observer. Like Chaucer in *The Canterbury Tales,* she presents portraits of other pilgrims and tells their stories. Hampl, however, also presents herself as seeking some spiritual illumination on her travels to a monastery in Assisi, the shrine in Lourdes, and a retreat house in northern California. Chapter Six of *Virgin Time*, originally published separately as an essay entitled "Parish Streets," is a reverie on that journey, a flashback in which we see the roots of Hampl's quest in her St. Paul, Minnesota, neighborhood.

Hampl describes the people in her neighborhood as having "dual citizenship." Like it or not, everyone lived along streets and in parishes. The streets—Oxford, Avon, Milton—and the parishes—St. Luke's, Nativity, Holy Spirit—name the same ground. Hampl uses the geography of her childhood to suggest that everyone, like it or not, must somehow come to terms with the questions religion poses. Even the agnostic Mrs. Krueger must work at it, because the reality of death and the longing for meaning lead us all to the questions, to the "problem." Hampl seems to agree with Mr. Bertram that "God isn't the problem." She defines the problem in other terms: "The perverse insubstantiality of the material world was the problem: reality refused to be real enough. . . . The clouds passing in the big sky kept dissipating, changing form. That was the problem."

Defining the problem in this way turns Hampl from reflections on the nature of God to reflections on how people devise ways of responding to constant, impersonal change. The churches of Hampl's childhood seemed inadequate to the task: her own Catholic church she says was "[f]ull of hair-splitting and odd rituals"; Lutherans were prone to "splice themselves into synods any which way"; Episcopalians were "snobbish"; Baptists feared the Vatican's influence on John Kennedy. The various denominations all seemed inordinately suspicious of each other. Hampl remarks on the "relentless xenophobia about other religions" that characterized her own church. Then, like so many in her generation, Hampl became "educated out of it all," never finding in the collection of churches around her coherence, common sense, compassion, or trust.

Virgin Time tells the story of Hampl's attempt to think again about the questions religion raises. She hopes this time to find the secret of the woman she saw many years before walking on Oxford Street each day. As she goes to school, Hampl passes the woman. They never speak, but Hampl describes her as "a person who prayed, who prayed alone, for no reason that I understood." And the praying seems to give her something. Unlike Mr. Bertram, "a resigned Buddha, looking up at the sky, which gave back nothing but drifting white shapes on the blue," this woman bows her head, and when she raises it to look at Hampl, "she shed light." Like Jimmy Giuliani, a bully in the schoolyard, she has something to offer Hampl. There is something energetic, vital in her look, and this is what Hampl seeks.

In the third part of *Virgin Time,* a section she calls "Silence," Hampl seems to find what she seeks in the contemplative life of some nuns at a retreat house in California. Silent contemplation characterizes her stay, which seems to be the culmination of her first steps on her quest, her visits to a monastery near her home in St. Paul. Then, she said, "silence was the first prayer I learned to trust"[2] and "The silence was God."[3] God, she asserted, "believed in or not remains only the elected Official for the colossal job of mystery. . . . [P]rayer, not the existence of God, is the thing to be decided."[4] And it is silent prayer, not the hearer of the prayers, that remains the focus of Hampl's retreat in California.

Experiences on Hampl's pilgrimages to Assisi and Lourdes, though, call into question the possibility of maintaining this focus outside the retreat house. God seems to be a problem on these journeys, and it is not clear how the silent contemplation of the retreat house will be able to resolve it. Twice on her pilgrimages, Hampl is asked directly whether or not she believes in God, first by a young guide on a hike near Assisi and then by a waiter in Lourdes. Hampl successfully evades the guide's question, prompting instead his confession: "I believe in poetry."[5] But the waiter in Lourdes will not be rebuffed by Hampl's attempts to avoid answering:

> I found myself not wishing to say *Yes, I believe.* Repelled by bringing the whole deep question to the surface of an *opinion*. . . .
> When I equivocated, he said impatiently, "One or the other, you either believe or you don't."
> "God, yes, I believe in God," I said, flustered, as if caving in to an impatient clerk who was fed up with my hesitation and demanded that I either take the goods or quit fingering them. But having said the words, I felt false, ripped off.[6]

In this awkward moment, Hampl makes an assertion of belief, but it is difficult for her to do so, and the silence of the retreat house does not seem to offer to ease this difficulty.

The silence, though, nurtures the prayer Hampl seeks, and so it offers her access to the power she finds in an unarticulated experience of God, in for instance, the smile of the woman who prayed as she walked along Oxford Street:

> When finally we were close enough to make eye contact, she looked up, straight into my face, and smiled. It was such a *complete* smile, so entire, it startled me every time, as if I'd heard my name called out on the street of a foreign city. (p. 69)

The smile has vitality and force. It seems to call out from a far-off foreign place, but the woman gives it no words. It remains mute, evocative but silent.

Paula J. Carlson

Notes

1. Patricia Hampl, *Virgin Time: In Search of the Contemplative Life* (New York: Farrar, Straus & Giroux, 1992).
2. *Virgin Time*, 35.
3. *Virgin Time*, 36.
4. *Virgin Time*, 35.
5. *Virgin Time*, 32.
6. *Virgin Time*, 175. Reprinted by permission of Farrar, Straus & Giroux, Inc.

Chapter 6 from *Virgin Time*

Lexington, Oxford, Chatsworth, continuing down Grand Avenue to Milton and Avon, as far as St. Albans—the streets of our neighborhood had an English, even an Anglican, ring to them. But we were Catholic. The parishes of the diocese, unmarked and ghostly as they were, posted borders more decisive than the street signs we passed on our way to St. Luke's grade school or, later, walking in the other direction to the girls-only convent high school.

We were like people with dual citizenship. I *lived* on Linwood Avenue, but I *belonged* to St. Luke's. That was the lingo. Mothers spoke of daughters who were going to the junior-senior prom with boys "from Nativity" or "from St. Mark's" as if from fiefdoms across the sea.

"Where you from?" a boy livid with acne asked when we startled each other lurking behind a pillar in the St. Thomas Academy gym at a Friday night freshman mixer.

"Ladies' choice!" one of the mothers cried from a dim corner where a portable hi-fi was set up. She rasped the needle over the vinyl, and Fats Domino came on, insinuating a heavier pleasure than I yet knew: *I found my thrill . . .*

"I'm from Holy Spirit," the boy said, as if he'd been beamed in to stand by the tepid Cokes and tuna sandwiches and the bowls of sweating potato chips on the refreshments table. Parish members did not blush to describe themselves as being "from Immaculate Conception." Somewhere north, near the city line, there was even a parish frankly named Maternity of Mary. But then, in those years, the 1950s and early 1960s, breeding was a low-grade fever pulsing among us unmentioned, like a buzz or hum you get used to and cease to hear. The white noise of matrimonial sex.

On Sundays the gray stone nave of St. Luke's Church, big as a warehouse, was packed with families of eight or ten sitting in the honeycolored pews. The fathers wore brown suits. In memory they appear spectrally thin, wraithlike and spent, like trees hollowed of their pulp. The wives were petite and cheerful, with helmet-like haircuts. Perkiness was their main trait. But what did they say, these small women, how did they talk? Mrs. Healy, mother of fourteen ("They can afford them," my mother said, as if to excuse her paltry two, "he's a doctor"), never uttered a word, as far as I remember. Even pregnant, she was somehow wiry, as if poised for a tennis match. Maybe these women only wore a *look* of perkiness, and like their lean husbands, they were sapped of personal strength. Maybe they were simply tense.

Not everyone around us was Catholic. Mr. Kirby, a widower who was our next-door neighbor, was Methodist—whatever that was. The Nugents across the street, behind their cement retaining wall and double row of giant salvia, were Lutheran, more or less. The Williams family, who subscribed to *The New Yorker* and had a living room outfitted with spare Danish furniture, were Episcopalian. They referred to their minister as a priest—a plagiarism that embarrassed me for them, because I liked them and their light, airy ways.

As for the Bertrams, our nearest neighbors to the west, it could only be said that Mrs. Bertram, dressed in a narrow suit with a peplum jacket and a hat made of the same heathery wool, went *somewhere* via taxi on Sunday mornings. Mr. Bertram went nowhere—on Sunday or on any other day. He was understood, during my entire girlhood, to be indoors, resting.

Weekdays, Mrs. Bertram took the bus to her job downtown. Mr. Bertram stayed home behind their birchwood Venetian blinds in an aquarium half-light, not an invalid (we never thought of him that way), but a man whose occupation it was to rest. Sometimes in the summer he ventured forth with a large wrench-like gadget to root out the masses of dandelions that gave the Bertrams' lawn a temporary brilliance in June. I associated him with the Wizard of Oz. He was small and mild-looking, going bald. He gave the impression of extreme pallor except for small, very dark eyes.

It was a solid neighborhood rumor that Mr. Bertram had been a screenwriter in Hollywood. Yes, that pallor was a writer's pallor; those small dark eyes were writer's eyes. They saw, they noted.

He allowed me to assist him in rooting out his dandelions. I wanted to ask him about Hollywood—had he met Audrey Hepburn? I couldn't bring myself to maneuver for information on such an elevated subject. But I did feel something serious was called for here. I introduced religion while he plunged the dandelion gadget deep into the lawn.

No, he said, he did not go to church. "But you do believe in God?" I asked, hardly daring to hope he did not. He paused for a moment and looked up at the sky, where big, spreading clouds streamed by. "God isn't the problem," he said.

Some ancient fissure split open, a fine crack in reality: so there *was* a problem. Just as I'd always felt. Beneath the family solidity, the claustrophobia of mother-father-brother-me, past the emphatic certainties of St.

Luke's catechism class, there was a problem that would never go away. Mr. Bertram stood amid his dandelions, a resigned Buddha, looking up at the sky, which gave back nothing but drifting white shapes on the blue.

What alarmed me was my feeling of recognition. Of course there was a problem. It wasn't God. Life itself was a problem. Something was not right, would never be right. I'd sensed it all along, a kind of fishy, vestigial quiver in the spine, way past thought. Life, deep down, lacked the substantiality it *seemed* to display. The physical world, full of detail and interest, was a parched topsoil that could be blown away.

This lack, this blankness akin to chronic disappointment, was everywhere, under the perkiness, lurking even within my own happiness. "What are you going to do today?" my father said when he saw me digging in the back yard on his way to work at the greenhouse.

"I'm digging to China," I said.

"Well, I'll see you at lunch," he said, "if you're still here."

I wouldn't bite. I frowned and went back to work with the bent tablespoon my mother had given me. It wasn't a game. I wanted out. I was on a desperate journey that only looked like play.

The blank disappointment, masked as weariness, played on the faces of people on the St. Clair bus. They looked out the windows, coming home from downtown, unseeing: clearly nothing interested them. What were they thinking of? The passing scene was not beautiful enough—was that it?—to catch their eye. Like the empty clouds Mr. Bertram turned to, their blank looks gave back nothing. There was an unshivered shiver in each of us, a shudder we managed to hold back.

We got off the bus at Oxford Street, where, one spring, in the lime-green house behind the catalpa tree on the corner, Mr. Lenart (whom we didn't know well) had slung a pair of tire chains over a rafter in the basement and hanged himself. Such things happened. Only the tight clutch of family life ("The family that prays together stays together") could keep things rolling along. Step out of the tight, bright circle, and you might find yourself dragging your chains down to the basement.

The perverse insubstantiality of the material world was the problem: reality refused to be real enough. Nothing could keep you steadfastly happy. That was clear. Some people blamed God. But I sensed that Mr. Bertram was right. *God isn't the problem.* The clouds passing in the big sky kept dissipating, changing form. That was the problem—but so what? Such worries resolved nothing, and were best left unworried—the unshivered shiver.

There was no one to blame. You could only retire, like Mr. Bertram, stay indoors behind your birchwood blinds and contemplate the impossibility of things, allowing the Hollywood glitter of reality to fade away and become a vague local rumor.

There were other ways of coping. Mrs. Krueger, several houses down with a big garden rolling with hydrangea bushes, held as her faith a passionate belief in knowledge. She sold World Book Encyclopedias. After trying Christian Science and a stint with the Unitarians, she had settled down as an agnostic. There seemed to be a lot of reading involved with being an agnostic, pamphlets and books, long citations on cultural anthropology in the World Book. It was an abstruse religion, and Mrs. Krueger seemed to belong to some ladies' auxiliary of disbelief.

But it didn't really matter what Mrs. Krueger decided about "the deity idea," as she called God. No matter what they believed, our neighbors lived not just on Linwood Avenue; they were in St. Luke's parish, too, whether they knew it or not. We claimed the territory. And we claimed them—even as we dismissed them. They were all non-Catholics, the term that disposed nicely of spiritual otherness.

Let the Protestants go down their schismatic paths; the Lutherans could splice themselves into synods any which way. Believers, non-believers, even Jews (the Kroners on the corner), or a breed as rare as the Greek Orthodox, whose church was across the street from St. Luke's—they were all non-Catholics, just so much extraneous spiritual matter orbiting the nether-sphere.

Or maybe it was more intimate than that, and we dismissed the rest of the world as we would our own serfs. We saw the Lutherans and Presbyterians, even those snobbish Episcopalians, as rude colonials, non-Catholics all, doing the best they could out there in the bush to imitate the ways of the homeland. We were the homeland.

Jimmy Giuliani was a bully. He pulled my hair when he ran by me on Oxford as we all walked home from St. Luke's, the girls like a midget army in navy jumpers and white blouses, the boys with the greater authority of free civilians without uniforms. They all wore pretty much the same thing anyway: corduroy pants worn smooth at the knees and flannel shirts, usually plaid.

I wasn't the only one Jimmy picked on. He pulled Moira Murphy's hair, he punched Tommy Hague. He struck without reason, indiscriminately, so full of violence it may have been pent-up enthusiasm released at random after the long day leashed in school. Catholic kids were alleged, by public school kids, to be mean fighters, dirty fighters. Jimmy Giuliani was the worst, a terror, hated and feared by Sister Julia's entire third-grade class.

So it came as a surprise when, after many weeks of his tyranny, I managed to land a sure kick to his groin and he collapsed in a heap and cried real tears. "You shouldn't *do* that to a boy," he said, whimpering. He was almost primly admonishing. "Do you know how that feels?"

It's not correct to say it was a sure kick. I just kicked. I took no aim and had no idea I'd hit paydirt—or why. Even when the tears started to his eyes and he doubled over clutching himself, I didn't understand.

But I liked it when he asked if I knew how it felt. For a brief, hopeful moment I thought he would tell me, that he would explain. Yes, tell me: how *does* it feel? And what's *there*, anyway? It was the first time the male body imposed itself.

I felt an odd satisfaction. I'd made contact. I wasn't glad I had hurt him, I wasn't even pleased to have taken the group's revenge on the class bully. I hadn't planned to kick him. It all just *happened*—as most physical encounters do. I was more astonished than he that I had succeeded in wounding him, I think. In a simple way, I wanted to say I was sorry. But I liked being taken seriously, and could not forfeit that rare pleasure by making an apology.

For a few weeks after I kicked him, I was in love with Jimmy Giuliani. Not because I'd hurt him, but because he had paused, looked right at me, and implored me to see things from his point of view. *Do you know how that feels?*

I didn't know—and yet I did. As soon as he asked, I realized obscurely that I did know how it felt. I knew what was there between his legs where he hurt. I ceased to be quite so ignorant. And sex began—with a blow.

The surprise of knowing what I hadn't realized I knew seemed beautifully private, but also illicit. That was a problem. I had no desire to be an outlaw. The way I saw it, you were supposed to know what you had been taught. This involved being given segments of knowledge by someone (usually a nun) designated to dole out information—strong medicine—in measured drams. Children were clean slates others were meant to write on.

But here was evidence that I was not a blank slate at all. I was scribbled all over with intuitions, premonitions, vague resonances clamoring to give their signals. I had caught Mr. Bertram's skyward look and its implicit promise: Life will be tough. There was no point in blaming God—the Catholic habit. Or even more Catholic, blaming the nuns, which allowed you to blame Mother and God all in one package.

And now, here was Jimmy Giuliani drawing out of me this other knowledge, bred of empathy and a swift kick to his balls. *Yes, I know how it feels.*

The hierarchy we lived in, a great linked chain of religious being, seemed set to control every entrance and exit to and from the mind and heart. The sky-blue Baltimore Catechism, small and square, read like an owner's manual for a very complicated vehicle. There was something pleasant, lulling and rhythmic, like heavily rhymed poetry, about the singsong Q-and-A format. Who would not give over heart, if not mind, to the brisk assurance of the Baltimore prose:

Who made you?
God made me.

Why did God make you?
God made me to know, love and serve Him in this world, in order to be happy with Him forever in the next.

And how harmless our Jesuitical discussions about what, exactly, constituted a meatless spaghetti sauce on Friday. Strict constructionists said no meat of any kind should ever, at any time, have made its way into the tomato sauce; easy liberals held with the notion that meatballs could be lurking around in the sauce, as long as you didn't eat them. My brother lobbied valiantly for the meatball, present but *intactus*. My mother said nothing doing. They raged for years.

Father Flannery, who owned his own airplane and drove a sports car, had given Peter some ammunition when he'd been asked to rule on the meatball question in the confessional. My mother would hear none of it. "I don't want to know what goes on between you and your confessor," she said, taking the high road.

"A priest, Ma, a *priest*," my brother cried. "This is an ordained priest saying right there in the sanctity of the confessional that meatballs are okay."

But we were going to heaven my mother's way.

Life was like that. Full of hair-splitting and odd rituals. We got our throats blessed on St. Blaise's day in February, the priest holding oversized beeswax candles in an X around our necks, to ward off death by choking on fishbones, a problem nobody thought of the rest of the year. There were smudged foreheads on Ash Wednesday, and home May altars with plaster statuettes of the Virgin festooned with lilacs. Advent wreaths and nightly family Rosary vigils during October (Rosary Month), all of us on our knees in the living room in front of the blank Magnavox.

The atmosphere swirled with the beatific visions and heroic martyrdoms of the long dead and the apocryphal. In grade school we were taken to daily Mass during Lent, and we read the bio notes of the saints that preceded the readings in the Daily Missal, learning that St. Agatha had

had her breasts cut off by the Romans. We thrilled at the word *breast,* pointing to it and giggling, as if it were a neon lingerie ad flashing from the prayerbook.

Most of the women saints in the Missal had under their names the designation *Virgin* and *Martyr,* as if the two categories were somehow a matched set. Occasionally a great female figure canonized for her piety and charitable works received the label *Queen* and *Widow.* The men were usually *Confessor* or, sometimes, *Martyr,* but none of them was ever *Virgin.*

The lives of the saints were not only edifying stories but cautionary tales. Chief here was St. Maria Goretti, early-twentieth-century *Virgin* and *Martyr,* who had been stabbed to death by a sex-crazed farmworker. She preserved her honor to the end. Her murderer, "alive to this day," we were told, had gone to her canonization in St. Peter's Square on his knees.

More troubling still was the story of Thomas à Kempis, the great author of *The Imitation of Christ,* one of the treasures of medieval scholasticism. Why, asked someone in Sister Hilaria's fifth-grade class, was Thomas à Kempis not *St. Thomas?*

Ah, Sister Hilaria said, pausing, looking at us to see if we were ready for this truth. We were ready.

Naturally, Sister said, there had been a canonization effort. All the usual procedures had been followed. Thomas was coming down the homestretch of the investigation when "very disturbing evidence was discovered." She paused again.

"The body of Thomas à Kempis was exhumed, children, as all such persons must be," Sister said reasonably. We nodded, we followed the macabre corporate ladder of sainthood without dismay. "When they opened that casket, boys and girls, Thomas à Kempis was lost." For upon opening the moldy box, there he was, the would-be saint, a ghastly look of horror on his wormy face, his hand clawing upward toward the air, madly. "You see, children, he did not die in the peace of the Lord." They shut him up and put him back. "A good man still," Sister said, "and a good writer." But not, we understood, a saint.

There were, as well, snatches of stories about nuns who beat kids with rulers in the coatroom; the priest who had a twenty-year affair with a member of the Altar and Rosary Society; the other priest in love with an altar boy—they'd had to send him away. Not St. Luke's stories—oh no, certainly not—but stories, floating, as stories do, from inner ear to inner ear, respecting no parish boundaries. Part of the ether.

And with it all, a relentless xenophobia about other religions. "It's going to be a mixed marriage, I understand," one of my aunts murmured about a friend's daughter who was marrying an Episcopalian. So what if he called himself High Church? He was a non-Catholic.

And now, educated out of it all, well climbed into the professions, the Catholics find each other at cocktail parties and get going. The nun stories, the first confession traumas—and a tone of rage and dismay that seems to bewilder even the tellers of these tales.

Nobody says, when asked, "I'm Catholic." It's always, "Yes, I was brought up Catholic." Anything to put it at a distance, to diminish the presence of that heritage which is not racial but acts as if it were. "You never get over it, you know," a fortyish lawyer told me a while ago at a party where we found ourselves huddled by the chips and dip, as if at a St. Thomas mixer once again.

He seemed to feel he was speaking to someone with the same hopeless congenital condition. "It's different now, of course," he said. "But when we were growing up back there . . . " There it was again: the past isn't a time. It's a place. A permanent destination: *back there*.

He had a very Jimmy Giuliani look to him. A chastened rascal. "I'm divorced," he said. We both smiled: there's no going to hell anymore. "Do they still have mortal sin?" he asked wistfully.

The love-hate lurch of a Catholic upbringing, like having an extra set of parents to contend with. Or an added national allegiance—not to the Vatican, as we were warned that the Baptists thought during John Kennedy's campaign for President. To a different realm. It was the implacable loyalty of faith, that flawless relation between self and existence into which we were born. A strange country where people prayed and believed impossible things.

The nuns who taught us, rigged up in their bold black habits with the big round wimples stiff as Frisbees, walked along our parish streets, moving from convent to church in twos or threes, dipping in the side door of the huge church "for a little adoration," as they would say. The roly-poly Irish-born monsignor told us to stand straight and proud when he met us slouching toward class along Summit. Fashionable Father Flannery took a companionable walk with the old pastor every night. The two of them took out white handkerchiefs and waved them for safety as they crossed the busy avenue on the way home in the dark, swallowed in their black suits and cassocks, lost in the growing gloom.

But the one I would like most to summon up and to have pass me on Oxford as I head off to St. Luke's in the early-morning mist, one of those mid-May weekdays, the lilacs just starting to spill, the one I want most to materialize from "back there"—I don't know her name, where, exactly, she lived, or who she was. We never spoke. We just passed each other, she coming home from six o'clock daily Mass, I going early to school to practice the piano for an hour before class began.

She was a "parish lady," part of the anonymous population that thickened our world, people who were always there, who were solidly part of us, part of what we were, but who never emerged beyond the bounds of being parishioners to become full-fledged persons.

We met every morning, just past the Healys' low brick wall. She wore a librarian's cardigan sweater. She must have been about forty-five, and I sensed she was not married. Unlike Dr. and Mrs. Harrigan, who walked smartly along Summit holding hands, their bright Irish setter accompanying them as far as the church door, where he waited till Mass was over, his tail thumping like a metronome on the pavement, the lady in the dust-colored cardigan was always alone.

I saw her coming all the way from Grand, where she had to pause for the traffic. She never rushed across the street, zipping past a truck, but waited until the coast was completely clear, and passed across keeping her floating pace. A peaceful gait, no rush to it. When finally we were close enough to make eye contact, she looked up, straight into my face, and smiled. It was such a *complete* smile, so entire, it startled me every time, as if I'd heard my name called out on the street of a foreign city.

She was a homely woman, plain and pale, unnoticeable. Her face seemed made of the same vague stuff as her sweater. But I felt—how to put it— she shed light. The mornings were often frail with mist, the light uncertain and tender. The smile was a brief flood of light. She loved me, I was sure.

I knew what it was about. She was praying. Her hand, stuck in her cardigan pocket, held one of the crystal beads of her rosary. I knew this. I'd once seen her take it out of the left pocket and quickly replace it after she had found the handkerchief she needed.

If I had seen a nun mumbling the Rosary along Summit (and this happened), it would not have meant much to me. But here on Oxford, the side street we used as a sleepy corridor to St. Luke's, it was a different thing. The parish lady was not a nun. She was a person who prayed, who prayed alone, for no reason that I understood. But there was no question that she prayed without ceasing, as the strange scriptural line instructed.

She didn't look up to the blank clouds for a response, as Mr. Bertram did in his stoic way. Her head was bowed, quite unconsciously. When she raised it, keeping her hand in her pocket where the clear beads were, she looked straight into the eyes of the person passing by. It was not an invasive look, but it latched. She had me. Not an intrusive gaze, but one brimming with a secret which, if only she had the words, it was clear she'd want to tell.

Guides to Reflection

1. During her reflection on Mr. Bertram's statement, Hampl says, "Of course there was a problem. It wasn't God. Life itself was a problem" (p. 63). All through her essay, Hampl keeps firm this distinction between God and life, that is, between God and human responses to what she presents as the central "problem" of life: mutability, that is, life is inconstant and prone to change. Think about the ways this distinction affects Hampl's view of God. What role does God seem to play in the lives of the people Hampl describes in her St. Paul neighborhood?

2. Hampl intertwines stories about sexuality with her stories about her neighbors' religious beliefs. She notes "[t]he white noise of matrimonial sex" (p. 61) when describing the babybooming families in her neighborhood; she remembers adolescent sexual awkwardness at high school dances; and she tells the story of her "sure kick" (p. 65) to Jimmy Giuliani's groin, when "sex began—with a blow" (p. 65). In what ways do you think the stories of sexuality and religious belief relate to each other? Why might Hampl have placed them together in this essay?

3. Some of the events and encounters Hampl tells of in the essay are set inside the church and some outside in the neighborhood. Consider the differences between the stories set in the two places. How do the differences illumine Hampl's view of God, "problem" or no?

4. Think about your own "pilgrimage" of faith. How is it like or different from that experienced by Hampl?

5. Do you find God or the existence of God to be a "problem"? Why or why not?

Raymond Carver

The landscape of Raymond Carver's fiction at first seems the last place to look for God. His America of motels, shopping malls, and foreclosed bungalows is a country without churches. And if his characters ever engage the subject of belief, ever ask one another if they "have a religion," the response is brief and negative: "I guess I don't believe in it. In anything. Sometimes it's hard. You know what I'm saying?"[1] Perhaps more powerfully than any other contemporary writer, Carver has described a post-Christian world in which faith in God has faded away almost without leaving a trace.

The characters who populate the author's six collections of short stories are modest, inarticulate people with few apparent resources. They work as waitresses, as door-to-door salesmen of vitamins or vacuum cleaners; they invariably come from somewhere else and keep on moving. No one has roots, nor does any one have quite enough money. By and large their aspirations are also small: they want simply to make the best of what they have, to make do with the "diminished thing" that is their life. Pleasures are also simple: people go fishing or visit friends, share meals, have sex, drink. Indeed, happiness seems to be most readily sought in alcohol, with its softening of edges and creation of quick (if ephemeral) intimacies.

So many of Carver's stories bring their characters to the edge of breakdown, as if to see how they will deal with forces they do not understand and cannot get a grip on. In "The Bridle," for instance, a man stakes everything he owns on a race horse, loses everything except the dream of winning next time, and then is forced to abandon even that final illusion. In "Vitamins," when a man returns home after an evening of betrayal and evasion, he discovers his wife in a state of hysteria and then takes refuge from her in the bathroom: "I couldn't take any more tonight. 'Go back to sleep, honey. I'm looking for something,' I said. I knocked some stuff out of the medicine chest. Things rolled into the sink. 'Where's the aspirin?' I said. I knocked down some more things. I didn't care. Things kept falling."[2]

Throughout Carver's fiction, characters find they cannot take anything more, cannot pick up all that is falling down around them. In language that is stripped down to the essentials, and in bone spare narratives that refuse to analyze the depths that they imply, the stories give us ordinary people who don't want much, but who nonetheless stand to lose their grip even on the little they have. Critics have accused Carver of cultivating despair, of creating a world in which these "hillbillies of the shopping mall" are all powerless to break out of their misfortune. Carver himself sees his characters as typically unable to meet their moral as well as financial responsibilities, but by no means as bankrupt. He brings them to a moment when they "realize that compromise, giving in, plays a major role in their lives."[3] In that instant of revelation the ordinary pattern of life is disrupted and possibility opened up. There is no guarantee, however, that revelation will lead to transformation. Compromise runs deep in Carver's characters, nor can they bear the pressure of very much reality. In "Feathers," for instance, a quietly miraculous evening shared by two couples leads to a sense of something perfect unfolding between them, a treasure to be held on to for a lifetime. And yet this moment of communion, whatever it means, cannot be sustained once the evening passes; nor can anyone talk about what was discovered or what lost. The couples simply never meet again, and so, "Mostly it's just the TV."

But there are other stories where something like real transformation occurs, when the door momentarily opens up between people and it seems as if it might stay open. In the course of "Cathedral," for instance, the fear and disdain that a man feels for a blind visitor to his home becomes a kind of love. In a simple but nonetheless extraordinary sequence of moves, he transcends his own boorishness to take on the reality of the other person, allowing himself, if only temporarily, also to become blind: "It was like nothing else in my life up till now."

This standing in the place of another person, this experience of deep sympathy between people who have been otherwise estranged, is Carver's secular equivalent of what Flannery O'Connor spoke of as "the almost imperceptible intrusions of grace."[4] Such moments of communion are all the more powerful for being so rare in his fiction. Certainly none is more poignant than the one portrayed in "A Small Good Thing." Here Carver tells the story of a little boy hit by a car on the morning of his birthday. The agony of his parents as they see their son fall into a coma is compounded by a series of bizarre calls to their home, requests to know why they have forgotten "about Scotty." Under the stress of the day they have neglected to pick up the cake ordered for their son's birthday; it is only after Scotty's death that they realize that the baker has made all those disturbing calls. Distraught by a loss they cannot yet begin to deal with, they then rush to the bakery with a thirst for revenge. And yet, once standing in the baker's forlorn presence, the mother's rage dwindles into a sense of helplessness.

Nor is she the only one affected: the news of the child's death, the passion of the mother, the grotesque inappropriateness of his telephoning—all these revelations work on the baker too, who for the first time seems to come out of the prison of himself. Confessing his loneliness and isolation ("I don't know how to act anymore"), he begs their forgiveness. The couple at first say nothing in response. Instead they allow the baker to feed them— "Eating is a small, good thing at a time like this"—and, as the three of them consume his fresh cinnamon rolls and coffee, they permit him to speak. Whereas the story opened with the man's refusal to talk, it concludes in a torrent of his self-revelation. Listening to him and eating his food, they then find themselves talking with the baker until dawn. Misery has brought them to his door "and they did not think of leaving."

In a profound moment of communication, Carver shows how hatred can turn to love, blindness to insight, and alienation into communion. There is nothing in the story that insists we take this moment of grace as anything more than "a small good thing," a miracle without God. And yet Carver also suggests the deeper mystery of human connection by leaving traces in his modest secular narrative of Christian sacred story. For as the baker feeds the couple with repeated urgings to take and eat, as former enemies join in table fellowship, there seems to be some faint memory of the Last Supper, some hint of a sacrament of reconciliation celebrated in the ordinary world. It is not necessary to call the baker's meal a Eucharist to acknowledge the mystery of his offering, the blessing discovered in the midst of utter loss. Perhaps it is enough to say that Carver gives us a powerful experience of communion between people and then lets us make of such small good things precisely what we will.

Peter S. Hawkins

Notes

1. Raymond Carver, "Cathedral," *Where I'm Calling From: New and Selected Stories* (New York: Random House, Vintage Books, 1989), 372.

2. "Vitamins," *Where I'm Calling From*, 263.

3. *Conversations with Raymond Carver*, eds. Marshall Bruce Gentry and William L. Stull (Jackson, Mississippi: University Press of Mississippi, 1990), 80.

4. Flannery O'Connor, *Mystery and Manners*, eds. Sally and Robert Fitzgerald (New York: Farrar, Straus & Giroux), 1974), 112.

A Small Good Thing

Saturday afternoon she drove to the bakery in the shopping center. After looking through a loose-leaf binder with photographs of cakes taped onto the pages, she ordered chocolate, the child's favorite. The cake she chose was decorated with a spaceship and launching pad under a sprinkling of white stars, and a planet made of red frosting at the other end. His name, SCOTTY, would be in green letters beneath the planet. The baker, who was an older man with a thick neck, listened without saying anything when she told him the child would be eight years old next Monday. The baker wore a white apron that looked like a smock. Straps cut under his arms, went around in back and then to the front again, where they were secured under his heavy waist. He wiped his hands on his apron as he listened to her. He kept his eyes down on the photographs and let her talk. He let her take her time. He'd just come to work and he'd be there all night, baking, and he was in no real hurry.

She gave the baker her name, Ann Weiss, and her telephone number. The cake would be ready on Monday morning, just out of the oven, in plenty of time for the child's party that afternoon. The baker was not jolly. There were no pleasantries between them, just the minimum exchange of words, the necessary information. He made her feel uncomfortable, and she didn't like that. While he was bent over the counter with the pencil in his hand, she studied his coarse features and wondered if he'd ever done anything else with his life besides be a baker. She was a mother and thirty-three years old, and it seemed to her that everyone, especially someone the baker's age—a man old enough to be her father—must have children who'd gone through this special time of cakes and birthday parties. There must be that between them, she thought. But he was abrupt with her— not rude, just abrupt. She gave up trying to make friends with him. She looked into the back of the bakery and could see a long, heavy wooden table with aluminum pie pans stacked at one end; and beside the table a metal container filled with empty racks. There was an enormous oven. A radio was playing country-western music.

The baker finished printing the information on the special order card and closed up the binder. He looked at her and said, "Monday morning."

She thanked him and drove home. On Monday morning, the birthday boy was walking to school with another boy. They were passing a bag of potato chips back and forth and the birthday boy was trying to find out what his friend intended to give him for his birthday that afternoon. Without looking, the birthday boy stepped off the curb at an intersection and was immediately knocked down by a car. He fell on his side with his head in the gutter and his legs out in the road. His eyes were closed, but his legs moved back and forth as if he were trying to climb over something. His friend dropped the potato chips and started to cry. The car had gone a hundred feet or so and stopped in the middle of the road. The man in the driver's seat looked back over his shoulder. He waited until the boy got unsteadily to his feet. The boy wobbled a little. He looked dazed, but okay. The driver put the car into gear and drove away.

The birthday boy didn't cry, but he didn't have anything to say about anything either. He wouldn't answer when his friend asked him what it felt like to be hit by a car. He walked home, and his friend went on to school. But after the birthday boy was inside his house and was telling his mother about it—she sitting beside him on the sofa, holding his hands in her lap, saying, "Scotty, honey, are you sure you feel all right, baby?" thinking she would call the doctor anyway—he suddenly lay back on the sofa, closed his eyes, and went limp. When she couldn't wake him up, she hurried to the telephone and called her husband at work. Howard told her to remain calm, remain calm, and then he called an ambulance for the child and left for the hospital himself.

Of course, the birthday party was canceled. The child was in the hospital with a mild concussion and suffering from shock. There'd been vomiting, and his lungs had taken in fluid which needed pumping out that afternoon. Now he simply seemed to be in a very deep sleep—but no coma, Dr. Francis had emphasized, no coma, when he saw the alarm in the parents' eyes. At eleven o'clock that night, when the boy seemed to be resting comfortably enough after the many X-rays and the lab work, and it was just a matter of his waking up and coming around, Howard left the hospital. He and Ann had been at the hospital with the child since that afternoon, and he was going home for a short while to bathe and change clothes. "I'll be back in an hour," he said. She nodded. "It's fine," she said. "I'll be right here." He kissed her on the forehead, and they touched hands. She sat in the chair beside the bed and looked at the child. She was waiting for him to wake up and be all right. Then she could begin to relax.

Howard drove home from the hospital. He took the wet, dark streets very fast, then caught himself and slowed down. Until now, his life had gone smoothly and to his satisfaction—college, marriage, another year of college for the advanced degree in business, a junior partnership in an investment firm. Fatherhood. He was happy and, so far, lucky—he knew that. His parents were still living, his brothers and his sister were established, his friends from college had gone out to take their places in the world. So far, he had kept away from any real harm, from those forces he knew existed and that could cripple or bring down a man if the luck went bad, if things suddenly turned. He pulled into the driveway and parked. His left leg began to tremble. He sat in the car for a minute and tried to deal with the present situation in a rational manner. Scotty had been hit by a car and was in the hospital, but he was going to be all right. Howard closed his eyes and ran his hand over his face. He got out of the car and went up to the front door. The dog was barking inside the house. The telephone rang and rang while he unlocked the door and fumbled for the light switch. He shouldn't have left the hospital, he shouldn't have. "Goddamn it!" he said. He picked up the receiver and said, "I just walked in the door!"

"There's a cake here that wasn't picked up," the voice on the other end of the line said.

"What are you saying?" Howard asked.

"A cake," the voice said. "A sixteen-dollar cake."

Howard held the receiver against his ear, trying to understand. "I don't know anything about a cake," he said. "Jesus, what are you talking about?"

"Don't hand me that," the voice said.

Howard hung up the telephone. He went into the kitchen and poured himself some whiskey. He called the hospital. But the child's condition remained the same; he was still sleeping and nothing had changed there. While water poured into the tub, Howard lathered his face and shaved. He'd just stretched out in the tub and closed his eyes when the telephone rang again. He hauled himself out, grabbed a towel, and hurried through the house, saying, "Stupid, stupid," for having left the hospital. But when he picked up the receiver and shouted, "Hello!" there was no sound at the other end of the line. Then the caller hung up.

He arrived back at the hospital a little after midnight. Ann still sat in the chair beside the bed. She looked up at Howard, and then she looked back at the child. The child's eyes stayed closed, the head was still wrapped in bandages. His breathing was quiet and regular. From an apparatus over the bed hung a bottle of glucose with a tube running from the bottle to the boy's arm.

"How is he?" Howard said. "What's all this?" waving at the glucose and the tube.

"Dr. Francis's orders," she said. "He needs nourishment. He needs to keep up his strength. Why doesn't he wake up, Howard? I don't understand, if he's all right."

Howard put his hand against the back of her head. He ran his fingers through her hair. "He's going to be all right. He'll wake up in a little while. Dr. Francis knows what's what."

After a time, he said, "Maybe you should go home and get some rest. I'll stay here. Just don't put up with this creep who keeps calling. Hang up right away."

"Who's calling?" she asked.

"I don't know who, just somebody with nothing better to do than call up people. You go on now."

She shook her head. "No," she said, "I'm fine."

"Really," he said. "Go home for a while, and then come back and spell me in the morning. It'll be all right. What did Dr. Francis say? He said Scotty's going to be all right. We don't have to worry. He's just sleeping now, that's all."

A nurse pushed the door open. She nodded at them as she went to the bedside. She took the left arm out from under the covers and put her fingers on the wrist, found the pulse, then consulted her watch. In a little while, she put the arm back under the covers and moved to the foot of the bed, where she wrote something on a clipboard attached to the bed.

"How is he?" Ann said. Howard's hand was a weight on her shoulder. She was aware of the pressure from his fingers.

"He's stable," the nurse said. Then she said, "Doctor will be in again shortly. Doctor's back in the hospital. He's making rounds right now."

"I was saying maybe she'd want to go home and get a little rest," Howard said. "After the doctor comes," he said.

"She could do that," the nurse said. "I think you should both feel free to do that, if you wish." The nurse was a big Scandinavian woman with blond hair. There was the trace of an accent in her speech.

"We'll see what the doctor says," Ann said. "I want to talk to the doctor. I don't think he should keep sleeping like this. I don't think that's a good sign." She brought her hand up to her eyes and let her head come forward a little. Howard's grip tightened on her shoulder, and then his hand moved up to her neck, where his fingers began to knead the muscles there.

"Dr. Francis will be here in a few minutes," the nurse said. Then she left the room.

Howard gazed at his son for a time, the small chest quietly rising and falling under the covers. For the first time since the terrible minutes after Ann's telephone call to him at his office, he felt a genuine fear starting in his limbs. He began shaking his head. Scotty was fine, but instead of sleeping at home in his own bed, he was in a hospital bed with bandages around his head and a tube in his arm. But this help was what he needed right now.

Dr. Francis came in and shook hands with Howard, though they'd just seen each other a few hours before. Ann got up from the chair. "Doctor?"

"Ann," he said and nodded. "Let's just first see how he's doing," the doctor said. He moved to the side of the bed and took the boy's pulse. He peeled back one eyelid and then the other. Howard and Ann stood beside the doctor and watched. Then the doctor turned back the covers and listened to the boy's heart and lungs with his stethoscope. He pressed his fingers here and there on the abdomen. When he was finished he went to the end of the bed and studied the chart. He noted the time, scribbled something on the chart, and then looked at Howard and Ann.

"Doctor, how is he?" Howard said. "What's the matter with him exactly?"

"Why doesn't he wake up?" Ann said.

The doctor was a handsome, big-shouldered man with a tanned face. He wore a three-piece blue suit, a striped tie, and ivory cuff links. His gray hair was combed along the sides of his head, and he looked as if he had just come from a concert. "He's all right," the doctor said. "Nothing to shout about, he could be better, I think. But he's all right. Still, I wish he'd wake up. He should wake up pretty soon." The doctor looked at the boy again. "We'll know some more in a couple of hours, after the results of a few more tests are in. But he's all right, believe me, except for the hairline fracture of the skull. He does have that."

"Oh, no," Ann said.

"And a bit of a concussion, as I said before. Of course, you know he's in shock," the doctor said. "Sometimes you see this in shock cases. This sleeping."

"But he's out of any real danger?" Howard said. "You said before he's not in a coma. You wouldn't call this a coma, then—would you, doctor?" Howard waited. He looked at the doctor.

"No, I don't want to call it a coma," the doctor said and glanced over at the boy once more. "He's just in a very deep sleep. It's a restorative measure the body is taking on its own. He's out of any real danger, I'd say that for certain, yes. But we'll know more when he wakes up and the other tests are in," the doctor said.

"It's a *coma*" Ann said. "Of sorts."

"It's not a coma yet, not exactly," the doctor said. "I wouldn't want to call it coma. Not yet, anyway. He's suffered shock. In shock cases, this kind of reaction is common enough; it's a temporary reaction to bodily trauma. Coma. Well, coma is a deep, prolonged unconsciousness, something that could go on for days, or weeks even. Scotty's not in that area, not as far as we can tell. I'm certain his condition will show improvement by morning. I'm betting that it will. We'll know more when he wakes up, which shouldn't be long now. Of course, you may do as you like, stay here or go home for a time. But by all means feel free to leave the hospital for a while if you want. This is not easy, I know." The doctor gazed at the boy again, watching him, and then he turned to Ann and said, "You try not to worry, little mother. Believe me, we're doing all that can be done. It's just a question of a little more time now." He nodded at her, shook hands with Howard again, and then he left the room.

Ann put her hand over the child's forehead. "At least he doesn't have a fever," she said. Then she said, "My God, he feels so cold, though. Howard? Is he supposed to feel like this? Feel his head."

Howard touched the child's temples. His own breathing had slowed. "I think he's supposed to feel this way right now," he said. "He's in shock, remember? That's what the doctor said. The doctor was just in here. He would have said something if Scotty wasn't okay."

Ann stood there a while longer, working her lip with her teeth. Then she moved over to her chair and sat down.

Howard sat in the chair next to her chair. They looked at each other. He wanted to say something else and reassure her, but he was afraid, too. He took her hand and put it in his lap, and this made him feel better, her hand being there. He picked up her hand and squeezed it. Then he just held her hand. They sat like that for a while, watching the boy and not talking. From time to time, he squeezed her hand. Finally, she took her hand away.

"I've been praying," she said.

He nodded.

She said, "I almost thought I'd forgotten how, but it came back to me. All I had to do was close my eyes and say, 'Please God, help us—help Scotty,' and then the rest was easy. The words were right there. Maybe if you prayed, too," she said to him.

"I've already prayed," he said. "I prayed this afternoon—yesterday afternoon, I mean—after you called, while I was driving to the hospital. I've been praying," he said.

"That's good," she said. For the first time, she felt they were together in it, this trouble. She realized with a start that, until now, it had only been happening to her and to Scotty.

She hadn't let Howard into it, though he was there and needed all along. She felt glad to be his wife.

The same nurse came in and took the boy's pulse again and checked the flow from the bottle hanging above the bed.

In an hour, another doctor came in. He said his name was Parsons, from Radiology. He had a bushy moustache. He was wearing loafers, a western shirt, and a pair of jeans.

"We're going to take him downstairs for more pictures," he told them. "We need to do some more pictures, and we want to do a scan."

"What's that?" Ann said. "A scan?" She stood between this new doctor and the bed. "I thought you'd already taken all your X-rays."

"I'm afraid we need some more," he said. "Nothing to be alarmed about. We just need some more pictures, and we want to do a brain scan on him."

"My God," Ann said.

"It's perfectly normal procedure in cases like this," this new doctor said. "We just need to find out for sure why he isn't back awake yet. It's normal medical procedure, and nothing to be alarmed about. We'll be taking him down in a few minutes," this doctor said.

In a little while, two orderlies came into the room with a gurney. They were black-haired, dark-complexioned men in white uniforms, and they said a few words to each other in a foreign tongue as they unhooked the boy from the tube and moved him from his bed to the gurney. Then they wheeled him from the room. Howard and Ann got on the same elevator. Ann gazed at the child. She closed her eyes as the elevator began its descent. The orderlies stood at either end of the gurney without saying anything, though once one of the men made a comment to the other in their own language, and the other man nodded slowly in response.

Later that morning, just as the sun was beginning to lighten the windows in the waiting room outside the X-ray department, they brought the boy out and moved him back up to his room. Howard and Ann rode up on the elevator with him once more, and once more they took up their places beside the bed.

They waited all day, but still the boy did not wake up. Occasionally, one of them would leave the room to go downstairs to the cafeteria to drink coffee and then, as if suddenly remembering and feeling guilty, get up from the table and hurry back to the room. Dr. Francis came again that afternoon and examined the boy once more and then left after telling them he was coming along and could wake up at any minute now. Nurses, different nurses from the night before, came in from time to time. Then a young woman from the lab knocked and entered the room. She wore white slacks and a white blouse and carried a little tray of things which she put on the stand beside the bed. Without a word to them, she took blood from the boy's arm. Howard closed his eyes as the woman found the right place on the boy's arm and pushed the needle in.

"I don't understand this," Ann said to the woman.

"Doctor's orders," the young woman said. "I do what I'm told. They say draw that one, I draw. What's wrong with him, anyway?" she said. "He's a sweetie."

"He was hit by a car," Howard said. "A hit-and-run."

The young woman shook her head and looked again at the boy. Then she took her tray and left the room.

"Why won't he wake up?" Ann said. "Howard? I want some answers from these people."

Howard didn't say anything. He sat down again in the chair and crossed one leg over the other. He rubbed his face. He looked at his son and then he settled back in the chair, closed his eyes, and went to sleep.

Ann walked to the window and looked out at the parking lot. It was night, and cars were driving into and out of the parking lot with their lights on. She stood at the window with her hands gripping the sill, and knew in her heart that they were into something now, something hard. She was afraid, and her teeth began to chatter until she tightened her jaws. She saw a big car stop in front of the hospital and someone, a woman in a long coat, get into the car. She wished she were that woman and somebody, anybody, was driving her away from here to somewhere else, a place where she would find Scotty waiting for her when she stepped out of the car, ready to say *Mom* and let her gather him in her arms.

In a little while, Howard woke up. He looked at the boy again. Then he got up from the chair, stretched, and went over to stand beside her at the window. They both stared out at the parking lot. They didn't say anything. But they seemed to feel each other's insides now, as though the worry had made them transparent in a perfectly natural way.

The door opened and Dr. Francis came in. He was wearing a different suit and tie this time. His gray hair was combed along the sides of his head, and he looked as if he had just shaved. He went straight to the bed and examined the boy.

"He ought to have come around by now. There's just no good reason for this," he said. "But I can tell you we're all convinced he's out of any danger. We'll just feel better when he wakes up. There's no reason, absolutely none, why he shouldn't come around. Very soon. Oh, he'll have himself a dilly of a headache when he does, you can count on that. But all of his signs are fine. They're as normal as can be."

"It is a *coma*, then?" Ann said.

The doctor rubbed his smooth cheek. "We'll call it that for the time being, until he wakes up. But you must be worn out. This is hard. I know this is hard. Feel free to go out for a bite," he said. "It would do you good. I'll put a nurse in here while you're gone if you'll feel better about going. Go and have yourselves something to eat."

"I couldn't eat anything," Ann said.

"Do what you need to do, of course," the doctor said. "Anyway, I wanted to tell you that all the signs are good, the tests are negative, nothing showed up at all, and just as soon as he wakes up he'll be over the hill."

"Thank you, doctor," Howard said. He shook hands with the doctor again. The doctor patted Howard's shoulder and went out.

"I suppose one of us should go home and check on things," Howard said. "Slug needs to be fed, for one thing."

"Call one of the neighbors," Ann said. "Call the Morgans. Anyone will feed a dog if you ask them to."

"All right," Howard said. After a while, he said, "Honey, why don't *you* do it? Why don't you go home and check on things, and then come back? It'll do you good. I'll be right here with him. Seriously," he said. "We need to keep up our strength on this. We'll want to be here for a while even after he wakes up."

"Why don't *you* go?" she said. "Feed Slug. Feed yourself."

"I already went," he said. "I was gone for exactly an hour and fifteen minutes. You go home for an hour and freshen up. Then come back."

She tried to think about it, but she was too tired. She closed her eyes and tried to think about it again. After a time, she said, "Maybe I *will* go home for a few minutes. Maybe if I'm not just sitting right here watching him every second, he'll wake up and be all right. You know? Maybe he'll wake up if I'm not here. I'll go home and take a bath and put on clean clothes. I'll feed Slug. Then I'll come back."

"I'll be right here," he said. "You go on home, honey. I'll keep an eye on things here." His eyes were bloodshot and small, as if he'd been drinking for a long time. His clothes were rumpled. His beard had come out again. She touched his face, and then she took her hand back. She understood he wanted to be by himself for a while, not have to talk or share his worry for a time. She picked her purse up from the nightstand, and he helped her into her coat.

"I won't be gone long," she said.

"Just sit and rest for a little while when you get home," he said. "Eat something. Take a bath. After you get out of the bath, just sit for a while and rest. It'll do you a world of good, you'll see. Then come back," he said. "Let's try not to worry. You heard what Dr. Francis said."

She stood in her coat for a minute trying to recall the doctor's exact words, looking for any nuances, any hint of something behind his words other than what he had said. She tried to remember if his expression had changed any when he bent over to examine the child. She remembered the way his features had composed themselves as he rolled back the child's eyelids and then listened to his breathing.

She went to the door, where she turned and looked back. She looked at the child, and then she looked at the father. Howard nodded. She stepped out of the room and pulled the door closed behind her.

She went past the nurses' station and down to the end of the corridor, looking for the elevator. At the end of the corridor, she turned to her right and entered a little waiting room where a Negro family sat in wicker chairs. There was a middle-aged man in a khaki shirt and pants, a baseball cap pushed back on his head. A large woman wearing a housedress and slippers was slumped in one of the chairs. A teenaged girl in jeans, hair done in dozens of little braids, lay stretched out in one of the chairs smoking a cigarette, her legs crossed at the ankles. The family swung their eyes to Ann as she entered the room. The little table was littered with hamburger wrappers and Styrofoam cups.

"Franklin," the large woman said as she roused herself. "Is it about Franklin?" Her eyes widened. "Tell me now, lady," the woman said. "Is it about Franklin?" She was trying to rise from her chair, but the man had closed his hand over her arm.

"Here, here," he said. "Evelyn."

"I'm sorry," Ann said. "I'm looking for the elevator. My son is in the hospital, and now I can't find the elevator."

"Elevator is down that way, turn left," the man said as he aimed a finger.

The girl drew on her cigarette and stared at Ann. Her eyes were narrowed to slits, and her broad lips parted slowly as she let the smoke escape. The Negro woman let her head fall on her shoulder and looked away from Ann, no longer interested.

"My son was hit by a car," Ann said to the man. She seemed to need to explain herself. "He has a concussion and a little skull fracture, but he's going to be all right. He's in shock now, but it might be some kind of coma, too. That's what really worries us, the coma part. I'm going out for a little while, but my husband is with him. Maybe he'll wake up while I'm gone."

"That's too bad," the man said and shifted in the chair. He shook his head. He looked down at the table, and then he looked back at Ann. She was still standing there. He said, "Our F anklin, he's on the operating table. Somebody cut him. Tried to kill him. There was a fight where he was at.

At this party. They say he was just standing and watching. Not bothering nobody. But that don't mean nothing these days. Now he's on the operating table. We're just hoping and praying, that's all we can do now." He gazed at her steadily.

Ann looked at the girl again, who was still watching her, and at the older woman, who kept her head down, but whose eyes were now closed. Ann saw the lips moving silently, making words. She had an urge to ask what those words were. She wanted to talk more with these people who were in the same kind of waiting she was in. She was afraid, and they were afraid. They had that in common. She would have liked to have said something else, about the accident, told them more about Scotty, that it had happened on the day of his birthday, Monday, and that he was still unconscious. Yet she didn't know how to begin. She stood looking at them without saying anything more.

She went down the corridor the man had indicated and found the elevator. She waited a minute in front of the closed doors, still wondering if she was doing the right thing. Then she put out her finger and touched the button.

She pulled into the driveway and cut the engine. She closed her eyes and leaned her head against the wheel for a minute. She listened to the ticking sounds the engine made as it began to cool. Then she got out of the car. She could hear the dog barking inside the house. She went to the front door, which was unlocked. She went inside and turned on lights and put on a kettle of water for tea. She opened some dog food and fed Slug on the back porch. The dog ate in hungry little smacks. It kept running into the kitchen to see that she was going to stay. As she sat down on the sofa with her tea, the telephone rang.

"Yes!" she said as she answered. "Hello!"

"Mrs. Weiss," a man's voice said. It was five o'clock in the morning, and she thought she could hear machinery or equipment of some kind in the background.

"Yes, yes! What is it?" she said. "This is Mrs. Weiss. This is she. What is it, please?" She listened to whatever it was in the background. "Is it Scotty, for Christ's sake?"

"Scotty," the man's voice said. "It's about Scotty, yes. It has to do with Scotty, that problem. Have you forgotten about Scotty?" the man said. Then he hung up.

She dialed the hospital's number and asked for the third floor. She demanded information about her son from the nurse who answered the telephone. Then she asked to speak to her husband. It was, she said, an emergency.

She waited, turning the telephone cord in her fingers. She closed her eyes and felt sick at her stomach. She would have to make herself eat. Slug came in from the back porch and lay down near her feet. He wagged his tail. She pulled at his ear while he licked her fingers. Howard was on the line.

"Somebody just called here," she said. She twisted the telephone cord. "He said it was about Scotty," she cried.

"Scotty's fine," Howard told her. "I mean, he's still sleeping. There's been no change. The nurse has been in twice since you've been gone. A nurse or else a doctor. He's all right."

"This man called. He said it was about Scotty," she told him.

"Honey, you rest for a little while, you need the rest. It must be that same caller I had. Just forget it. Come back down here after you've rested. Then we'll have breakfast or something."

"Breakfast," she said. "I don't want any breakfast."

"You know what I mean," he said. "Juice, something. I don't know. I don't know anything, Ann. Jesus, I'm not hungry, either. Ann, it's hard to talk now. I'm standing here at the desk. Dr. Francis is coming again at eight o'clock this morning. He's going to have something to tell us then, something more definite. That's what one of the nurses said. She didn't know any more than that. Ann? Honey, maybe we'll know something more then. At eight o'clock. Come back here before eight. Meanwhile, I'm right here and Scotty's all right. He's still the same," he added.

"I was drinking a cup of tea," she said, "when the telephone rang. They said it was about Scotty. There was a noise in the background. Was there a noise in the background on that call you had, Howard?"

"I don't remember," he said. "Maybe the driver of the car, maybe he's a psychopath and found out about Scotty somehow. But I'm here with him. Just rest like you were going to do. Take a bath and come back by seven or so, and we'll talk to the doctor together when he gets here. It's going to be all right, honey. I'm here, and there are doctors and nurses around. They say his condition is stable."

"I'm scared to death," she said.

She ran water, undressed, and got into the tub. She washed and dried quickly, not taking the time to wash her hair. She put on clean underwear, wool slacks, and a sweater. She went into the living room, where the dog looked up at her and let its tail thump once against the floor. It was just starting to get light outside when she went out to the car.

She drove into the parking lot of the hospital and found a space close to the front door. She felt she was in some obscure way responsible for what had happened to the child. She let her thoughts move to the Negro family. She remembered the name Franklin and the table that was covered with hamburger papers, and the teenaged girl staring at her as she drew on her cigarette. "Don't have children," she told the girl's image as she entered the front door of the hospital. "For God's sake, don't."

She took the elevator up to the third floor with two nurses who were just going on duty. It was Wednesday morning, a few minutes before seven. There was a page for a Dr. Madison as the elevator doors slid open on the third floor. She got off behind the nurses, who turned in the other direction and continued the conversation she had interrupted when she'd gotten into the elevator. She walked down the corridor to the little alcove where the Negro family had been waiting. They were gone now, but the chairs were scattered in such a way that it looked as if people had just jumped up from them the minute before. The tabletop was cluttered with the same cups and papers, the ashtray was filled with cigarette butts.

She stopped at the nurses' station. A nurse was standing behind the counter, brushing her hair and yawning.

"There was a Negro boy in surgery last night," Ann said. "Franklin was his name. His family was in the waiting room. I'd like to inquire about his condition."

A nurse who was sitting at a desk behind the counter looked up from a chart in front of her. The telephone buzzed and she picked up the receiver, but she kept her eyes on Ann. "He passed away," said the nurse at the counter. The nurse held the hairbrush and kept looking at her. "Are you a friend of the family or what?"

"I met the family last night," Ann said. "My own son is in the hospital. I guess he's in shock. We don't know for sure what's wrong. I just wondered about Franklin, that's all. Thank you." She moved down the corridor. Elevator doors the same color as the walls slid open and a gaunt, bald man in white pants and white canvas shoes pulled a heavy cart off the elevator. She hadn't noticed these doors last night. The man wheeled the cart out into the corridor and stopped in front of the room nearest the elevator and consulted a clipboard. Then he reached down and slid a tray out of the cart. He rapped lightly on the door and entered the room. She could smell the unpleasant odors of warm food as she passed the cart. She hurried on without looking at any of the nurses and pushed open the door to the child's room.

Howard was standing at the window with his hands behind his back. He turned around as she came in.

"How is he?" she said. She went over to the bed. She dropped her purse on the floor beside the nightstand. It seemed to her she had been gone a long time. She touched the child's face. "Howard?"

"Dr. Francis was here a little while ago," Howard said. She looked at him closely and thought his shoulders were bunched a little.

"I thought he wasn't coming until eight o'clock this morning," she said quickly.

"There was another doctor with him. A neurologist."

"A neurologist," she said.

Howard nodded. His shoulders were bunching, she could see that. "What'd they say, Howard? For Christ's sake, what'd they say? What is it?"

"They said they're going to take him down and run more tests on him, Ann. They think they're going to operate, honey. Honey, they are going to operate. They can't figure out why he won't wake up. It's more than just shock or concussion, they know that much now. It's in his skull, the fracture, it has something, something to do with that, they think. So they're going to operate. I tried to call you, but I guess you'd already left the house."

"Oh, God," she said. "Oh, please, Howard, please," she said, taking his arms.

"Look!" Howard said. "Scotty! Look, Ann!" He turned her toward the bed.

The boy had opened his eyes, then closed them. He opened them again now. The eyes stared straight ahead for a minute, then moved slowly in his head until they rested on Howard and Ann, then traveled away again.

"Scotty," his mother said, moving to the bed.

"Hey, Scott," his father said. "Hey, son."

They leaned over the bed. Howard took the child's hand in his hands and began to pat and squeeze the hand. Ann bent over the boy and kissed his forehead again and again. She put her hands on either side of his face. "Scotty, honey, it's Mommy and Daddy," she said. "Scotty?"

The boy looked at them, but without any sign of recognition. Then his mouth opened, his eyes scrunched closed, and he howled until he had no more air in his lungs. His face seemed to relax and soften then. His lips parted as his last breath was puffed through his throat and exhaled gently through the clenched teeth.

The doctors called it a hidden occlusion, and said it was a one-in-a-million circumstance. Maybe if it could have been detected somehow and surgery undertaken immediately, they could have saved him. But more than likely not. In any case, what would they have been looking for? Nothing had shown up in the tests or in the X-rays.

Dr. Francis was shaken. "I can't tell you how badly I feel. I'm so very sorry, I can't tell you," he said as he led them into the doctors' lounge. There was a doctor sitting in a chair with his legs hooked over the back of another chair, watching an early-morning TV show. He was wearing a green delivery-room outfit, loose green pants and green blouse, and a green cap that covered his hair. He looked at Howard and Ann and then looked at Dr. Francis. He got to his feet and turned off the set and went out of the room. Dr. Francis guided Ann to the sofa, sat down beside her, and began to talk in a low, consoling voice. At one point, he leaned over and embraced her. She could feel his chest rising and falling evenly against her shoulder. She kept her eyes open and let him hold her. Howard went into the bathroom, but he left the door open. After a violent fit of weeping, he ran water and washed his face. Then he came out and sat down at the little table that held a telephone. He looked at the telephone as though deciding what to do first. He made some calls. After a time, Dr. Francis used the telephone.

"Is there anything else I can do for the moment?" he asked them.

Howard shook his head. Ann stared at Dr. Francis as if unable to comprehend his words.

The doctor walked them to the hospital's front door. People were entering and leaving the hospital. It was eleven o'clock in the morning. Ann was aware of how slowly, almost reluctantly, she moved her feet. It seemed to her that Dr. Francis was making them leave when she felt they should stay, when it would be more the right thing to do to stay. She gazed out into the parking lot and then turned around and looked back at the front of the hospital. She began shaking her head. "No, no," she said. "I can't leave him here, no." She heard herself say that and thought how unfair it was that the only words that came out were the sort of words used on TV shows where people were stunned by violent or sudden deaths. She wanted her words to be her own. "No," she said, and for some reason the memory of the Negro woman's head lolling on the woman's shoulder came to her. "No," she said again.

"I'll be talking to you later in the day," the doctor was saying to Howard. "There are still some things that have to be done, things that have to be cleared up to our satisfaction. Some things that need explaining."

"An autopsy," Howard said.

Dr. Francis nodded.

"I understand," Howard said. Then he said, "Oh, Jesus."

"No, I don't understand, doctor. I can't, I can't. I just can't."

Dr. Francis put his arm around Howard's shoulders. "I'm sorry. God, how I'm sorry." He let go of Howard's shoulders and held out his hand. Howard looked at the hand, and then he took it. Dr. Francis put his arms around Ann once more. He seemed full of some goodness she didn't understand. She let her head rest on his shoulder, but her eyes stayed open. She kept looking at the hospital. As they drove out of the parking lot, she looked back at the hospital.

At home, she sat on the sofa with her hands in her coat pockets. Howard closed the door to the child's room. He got the coffee-maker going and then he found an empty box. He had thought to pick up some of the child's things that were scattered around the living room. But instead he sat down beside her on the sofa, pushed the box to one side, and leaned forward, arms between his knees. He began to weep. She pulled his head over into her lap and patted his shoulder. "He's gone," she said. She kept patting his shoulder. Over his sobs, she could hear the coffee-maker hissing in the kitchen. "There, there," she said tenderly. "Howard, he's gone. He's gone and now we'll have to get used to that. To being alone."

In a little while, Howard got up and began moving aimlessly around the room with the box, not putting anything into it, but collecting some things together on the floor at one end of the sofa. She continued to sit with her hands in her coat pockets. Howard put the box down and brought coffee into the living room. Later, Ann made calls to relatives. After each call had been placed and the party had answered, Ann would blurt out a few words and cry for a minute. Then she would quietly explain, in a measured voice, what had happened and tell them about arrangements. Howard took the box out to the garage, where he saw the child's bicycle. He dropped the box and sat down on the pavement beside the bicycle. He took hold of the bicycle awkwardly so that it leaned against his chest. He held it, the rubber pedal sticking into his chest. He gave the wheel a turn.

Ann hung up the telephone after talking to her sister. She was looking up another number when the telephone rang. She picked it up on the first ring.

"Hello," she said, and she heard something in the background, a humming noise. "Hello!" she said. "For God's sake," she said. "Who is this? What is it you want?"

"Your Scotty, I got him ready for you," the man's voice said. "Did you forget him?"

"You evil bastard!" she shouted into the receiver. "How can you do this, you evil son of a bitch?"

"Scotty," the man said. "Have you forgotten about Scotty?" Then the man hung up on her.

Howard heard the shouting and came in to find her with her head on her arms over the table, weeping. He picked up the receiver and listened to the dial tone.

Much later, just before midnight, after they had dealt with many things, the telephone rang again.

"You answer it," she said. "Howard, it's him, I know." They were sitting at the kitchen table with coffee in front of them. Howard had a small glass of whiskey beside his cup. He answered on the third ring.

"Hello," he said. "Who is this? Hello! Hello!" The line went dead. "He hung up," Howard said. "Whoever it was."

"It was him," she said. "That bastard. I'd like to kill him," she said. "I'd like to shoot him and watch him kick," she said.

"Ann, my God," he said.

"Could you hear anything?" she said. "In the background? A noise, machinery, something humming?"

"Nothing, really. Nothing like that," he said. "There wasn't much time. I think there was some radio music. Yes, there was a radio going, that's all I could tell. I don't know what in God's name is going on," he said.

She shook her head. "If I could, could get my hands on him." It came to her then. She knew who it was. Scotty, the cake, the telephone number. She pushed the chair away from the table and got up. "Drive me down to the shopping center," she said. "Howard."

"What are you saying?"

"The shopping center. I know who it is who's calling. I know who it is. It's the baker, the son-of-a-bitching baker, Howard. I had him bake a cake for Scotty's birthday. That's who's calling. That's who has the number and keeps calling us. To harass us about that cake. The baker, that bastard." They drove down to the shopping center. The sky was clear and stars were out. It was cold, and they ran the heater in the car. They parked in front of the bakery. All of the shops and stores were closed, but there were cars at the far end of the lot in front of the movie theater. The bakery windows were dark, but when they looked through the glass they could see a light in the back room and, now and then, a big man in an apron moving in and out of the white, even light. Through the glass, she could see the display cases and some little tables with chairs. She tried the door. She rapped on the glass. But if the baker heard them, he gave no sign. He didn't look in their direction.

They drove around behind the bakery and parked. They got out of the car. There was a lighted window too high up for them to see inside. A sign near the back door said THE PANTRY BAKERY, SPECIAL ORDERS. She could hear faintly a radio playing inside and something creak—an oven door as it was pulled down? She knocked on the door and waited. Then she knocked again, louder. The radio was turned down and there was a scraping sound now, the distinct sound of something, a drawer, being pulled open and then closed.

Someone unlocked the door and opened it. The baker stood in the light and peered out at them. "I'm closed for business," he said. "What do you want at this hour? It's midnight. Are you drunk or something?"

She stepped into the light that fell through the open door. He blinked his heavy eyelids as he recognized her. "It's you," he said.

"It's me," she said. "Scotty's mother. This is Scotty's father. We'd like to come in."

The baker said, "I'm busy now. I have work to do."

She had stepped inside the doorway anyway. Howard came in behind her. The baker moved back. "It smells like a bakery in here. Doesn't it smell like a bakery in here, Howard?"

"What do you want?" the baker said. "Maybe you want your cake? That's it, you decided you want your cake. You ordered a cake, didn't you?"

"You're pretty smart for a baker," she said. "Howard, this is the man who's been calling us." She clenched her fists. She stared at him fiercely. There was a deep burning inside her, an anger that made her feel larger than herself, larger than either of these men.

"Just a minute here," the baker said. "You want to pick up your three-day-old cake? That it? I don't want to argue with you, lady. There it sits over there, getting stale. I'll give it to you for half of what I quoted you. No. You want it? You can have it. It's no good to me, no good to anyone now. It cost me time and money to make that cake. If you want it, okay, if you don't, that's okay, too. I have to get back to work." He looked at them and rolled his tongue behind his teeth.

"More cakes," she said. She knew she was in control of it, of what was increasing in her. She was calm.

"Lady, I work sixteen hours a day in this place to earn a living," the baker said. He wiped his hands on his apron. "I work night and day in here, trying to make ends meet." A look crossed Ann's face that made the baker move back and say, "No trouble, now." He reached to the counter and picked up a rolling pin with his right hand and began to tap it against the palm of his other hand. "You want the cake or not? I have to get back to work. Bakers work at night," he said again. His eyes were small, mean-looking, she thought, nearly lost in the bristly flesh around his cheeks. His neck was thick with fat.

"I know bakers work at night," Ann said. "They make phone calls at night, too. You bastard," she said.

The baker continued to tap the rolling pin against his hand. He glanced at Howard. "Careful, careful," he said to Howard.

"My son's dead," she said with a cold, even finality. "He was hit by a car Monday morning. We've been waiting with him until he died. But, of course, you couldn't be expected to know that, could you? Bakers can't know everything—can they Mr. Baker? But he's dead. He's dead, you bastard!" Just as suddenly as it had welled in her, the anger dwindled, gave way to something else, a dizzy feeling of nausea. She leaned against the wooden table that was sprinkled with flour, put her hands over her face, and began to cry, her shoulders rocking back and forth. "It isn't fair," she said. "It isn't, isn't fair."

Howard put his hand at the small of her back and looked at the baker. "Shame on you," Howard said to him. "Shame."

The baker put the rolling pin back on the counter. He undid his apron and threw it on the counter. He looked at them, and then he shook his head slowly. He pulled a chair out from under the card table that held papers and receipts, an adding machine, and a telephone directory. "Please sit down," he said. "Let me get you a chair," he said to Howard.

"Sit down now, please." The baker went into the front of the shop and returned with two little wrought-iron chairs. "Please sit down, you people."

Ann wiped her eyes and looked at the baker. "I wanted to kill you," she said. "I wanted you dead."

The baker had cleared a space for them at the table. He shoved the adding machine to one side, along with the stacks of notepaper and receipts. He pushed the telephone directory onto the floor, where it landed with a thud. Howard and Ann sat down and pulled their chairs up to the table. The baker sat down, too.

"Let me say how sorry I am," the baker said, putting his elbows on the table. "God alone knows how sorry. Listen to me. I'm just a baker. I don't claim to be anything else. Maybe once, maybe years ago, I was a different kind of human being. I've forgotten, I don't know for sure. But I'm not any longer, if I ever was. Now I'm just a baker. That don't excuse my doing what I did, I know. But I'm deeply sorry. I'm sorry for your son, and sorry for my part in this," the baker said. He spread his hands out on the table and turned them over to reveal his palms. "I don't have any children myself, so I can only imagine what you must be feeling. All I can say to you now is that I'm sorry. Forgive me, if you can," the baker said. "I'm not an evil man, I don't think. Not evil, like you said on the phone. You got to understand what it comes down to is I don't know how to act anymore, it would seem. Please," the man said, "let me ask you if you can find it in your hearts to forgive me?"

It was warm inside the bakery. Howard stood up from the table and took off his coat. He helped Ann from her coat. The baker looked at them for a minute and then nodded and got up from the table. He went to the oven and turned off some switches. He found cups and poured coffee from an electric coffee-maker. He put a carton of cream on the table, and a bowl of sugar.

"You probably need to eat something," the baker said. "I hope you'll eat some of my hot rolls. You have to eat and keep going. Eating is a small good thing at a time like this," he said.

He served them warm cinnamon rolls just out of the oven, the icing still runny. He put butter on the table and knives to spread the butter. Then the baker sat down at the table with them. He waited. He waited until they each took a roll from the platter and began to eat. "It's good to eat something," he said, watching them. "There's more. Eat up. Eat all you want. There's all the rolls in the world here."

They ate rolls and drank coffee. Ann was suddenly hungry, and the rolls were warm and sweet. She ate three of them, which pleased the baker. Then he began to talk. They listened carefully. Although they were tired and in anguish, they listened to what the baker had to say. They nodded when the baker began to speak of loneliness, and of the sense of doubt and limitation that had come to him in his middle years. He told them what it was like to be childless all these years. To repeat the days with the ovens endlessly full and endlessly empty. The party food, the celebrations he'd worked over. Icing knuckle-deep. The tiny wedding couples stuck into cakes. Hundreds of them, no, thousands by now. Birthdays. Just imagine all those candles burning. He had a necessary trade. He was a baker. He was glad he wasn't a florist. It was better to be feeding people. This was a better smell anytime than flowers.

"Smell this," the baker said, breaking open a dark loaf. "It's a heavy bread, but rich." They smelled it, then he had them taste it. It had the taste of molasses and coarse grains. They listened to him. They ate what they could. They swallowed the dark bread. It was like daylight under the fluorescent trays of light. They talked on into the early morning, the high, pale cast of light in the windows, and they did not think of leaving.

Guides to Reflection

1. Carver's story both begins and ends with the figure of the baker in his shopping center bakery. At the outset he says only, "Good morning," but as the story reaches its climax he opens himself up in a torrent of speech. What exactly has happened? What experiences have given him his voice? What other examples are present in the story whereby characters find release through words, simply by being moved to share their pain?

2. When Anne Weiss, Scotty's mother, heads for the shopping center bakery with murder in her heart, she is clearly displacing her enormous sense of grief: if she cannot bring her son back from the dead, she can at least make the baker suffer for the additional pain his unknowing telephone calls caused her. At the peak of her rage, however, we are told that "[just] as suddenly as it had welled in her, the anger dwindled, gave way to something else." What causes this change? What is it that enables this bereaved woman and her husband not only to listen to the baker but to talk with him until dawn? How do you account for the profound change in both of them?

3. Carver has said, "I don't know if I believe in God, but I do believe in miracles." How does a reader who does, in fact, believe in God experience "A Small Good Thing"? Guarding against the tendency to turn it into what we might want it to be or to say, what might a genuinely *religious* interpretation of this story be? Discuss the implications of finding Christian meaning in work that may have no Christian intent behind it.

4. The hospital stands at the center of this story, even though its major scene takes place in the bakery. Given your own experience, how does Carver portray doctors and nurses, the hardship of waiting for medical information and diagnosis, the relationships that can spring up momentarily between people dealing with private pain?

5. If you are willing, please share an experience of personal grieving or of ministering to someone else who was in grief. What role did faith play in this experience?

Annie Dillard

In her memoir *An American Childhood*, Annie Dillard tells a story of being chased for blocks by a man whose car she and some friends had thrown snowballs at one winter morning. Dillard, seven years old then, ran through backyards and between narrow hedges, across alleys and under low trees, up hills and down steps in an exhausting attempt to escape the relentless man. Running until she could run no more, Dillard found the chase exhilarating. She admired the man. She says that as he ran, refusing to quit, he showed her something: "It was an immense discovery, pounding into my hot head with every sliding, joyous step, that this ordinary adult evidently knew what I thought only children trained at football knew: that you have to fling yourself at what you're doing, you have to point yourself, forget yourself, aim, dive."[1]

The scolding the man gives Dillard and her friend when he catches them is anticlimactic. It was, Dillard says, "beside the point." Instead, the chase is what mattered: "The point was that he had chased us passionately without giving up, and so he had caught us."[2]

The passionate engagement that Dillard finds so compelling in the running man is the most distinctive feature of the many books of prose and poetry that she has written, beginning with *Tickets for a Prayer Wheel* and *Pilgrim at Tinker Creek*. Dillard's intense, sometimes fierce gaze at nature characterizes the reflective essays in *Pilgrim*, for which she won a Pulitzer Prize in 1975. Like Ralph Waldo Emerson, Henry David Thoreau, and William Wordsworth before her, Dillard wanders the countryside, turns her eye to nature, and then reflects in her writing on the beauty and power she finds there. For Dillard, nature offers great joy and elicits profound wonder, but it raises disturbing questions as well. Nature can awe Dillard, but it can also terrify her.

In *Pilgrim*, Dillard describes frogs jumping along Tinker Creek in the summer. She notices the rich green of the grass and the frogs; she delights in the jumping and croaking of the creatures; she watches the reflected sunlight change texture in the grass, the frogs, and the creek. And then she sees a frog, lying still, partly in and partly out of the water:

He was a very small frog with wide, dull eyes. And just as I looked at him, he slowly crumpled and began to sag. The spirit vanished from his eyes as if snuffed. His skin emptied and drooped; his very skull seemed to collapse and settle like a kicked tent. He was shrinking before my eyes like a deflating football. I watched the taut, glistening skin on his shoulders ruck, and rumple, and fall. Soon, part of his skin, formless as a pricked balloon, lay in floating folds like bright scum on top of the water: it was a monstrous and terrifying thing.[3]

The frog has been eaten by a giant water bug, a creature that sucks the insides out of frogs, fish, and tadpoles.

Dillard finds such sights in nature profoundly disquieting. In her essays, she asks what kind of God would create a world with such beauty and such terror, a world having what she calls "a grace wholly gratuitous"[4] and, at the same time, a ruthless cruelty in its everyday, ordinary ways. What kind of world is this?—a world of "grace tangled in a rapture with violence"?[5] Why would God do this?

Dillard's relentless questioning and her unflinching gaze lead her to struggle with problems that bewilder and with issues that resist resolution. Suffering, evil, death. The nature of God. The mystery of love. For Dillard, art becomes the means of describing the reality, posing the questions, and articulating what response is possible:

> Art itself is an instrument, a cognitive instrument, and with religion the only instrument, for probing certain materials and questions. Art and religion probe the mysteries in those difficult areas where blurred and powerful symbols are the only possible speech and their arrangement into coherent religions and works of art the only possible grammar.[6]

Dillard includes in her "grammar" the realities of beauty and terror, the difficulties of suffering and pain, and the hope that the power and love of God will overcome the evil and terror she sees with such clarity and describes with such force.

Dillard's hope endures despite the difficulty of knowing God, despite the impossibility of fully understanding God's will. Dillard asserts in *Holy the Firm*, her long essay about the suffering of a young girl and the inscrutability of God, that "I know only enough of God to want to worship him, by any means ready to hand."[7] But that desire to worship comes without complete comprehension. It comes even though God is often silent, mysterious, and frightening. It comes despite Dillard's inability to understand, for instance, why the captured deer and the burned man she writes about in "The Deer at Providencia" suffer. In "Teaching a Stone to Talk," Dillard describes the attempt of a neighbor to speak with a stone. Like this man, Dillard goes to nature to try to hear something. She strains to hear the voice of God. Most often, though, there is only silence: "But you wait, you give your life's length to listening, and nothing happens."[8]

When God does speak, when, for instance, Dillard suddenly one day perceived angels whirling in a field and "heard" God talk to her, she "turned away, willful." "Hearing" the voice of God, "seeing" the angels frightens her. Like the religious mystics who for centuries have written of extraordinary experiences of God, Dillard describes for her readers these moments of powerful connection with God. She finds in them a strong basis for belief, but she refuses to assume too much of them: "What all this means about perception, or language, or angels, or my own sanity, I have no idea." God remains inscrutable even in revelation, and she turns away even when God comes in love:

> I am still running, running from that knowledge, that eye, that love from which there is no refuge. For you meant only love, and love, and I felt only fear, and pain. So once in Israel love came to us incarnate, stood in the doorway between two worlds, and we were all afraid."[9]

God's power and majesty, like God's silence, can seem overwhelming to Dillard. In silence or in revelation, God exceeds the human capacity to understand, and Dillard cannot in either case fully "know" God. She can, she says, "know only enough of God to want to worship him."[10]

Despite the limitations she encounters, Dillard continues to probe the enigmas of nature and theology. And like the running man of her Pittsburgh childhood, Dillard flings herself at her task. Her essays give her readers a powerful, compelling means of pointing themselves, aiming, and diving into that passionate quest with her.

Paula J. Carlson

Notes

1. Annie Dillard, *An American Childhood* (New York: Harper and Row, 1987), 47.
2. *An American Childhood*, 48.
3. Annie Dillard, *Pilgrim at Tinker Creek* (New York: Harper and Row, 1974), 5-6.
4. *Pilgrim at Tinker Creek*, 7.
5. *Pilgrim at Tinker Creek*, 8.
6. Annie Dillard, *Living by Fiction* (New York: Harper and Row, 1982), 164.
7. Annie Dillard, *Holy the Firm* (New York: Harper and Row, 1977), 55.
8. Annie Dillard, *Teaching a Stone to Talk* (New York: Harper and Row, 1982), 72.
9. "God in the Doorway" in *Teaching a Stone to Talk*, 141.
10. *Holy the Firm*, 55.

The Deer at Providencia

There were four of us North Americans in the jungle, in the Ecuadorian jungle on the banks of the Napo River in the Amazon watershed. The other three North Americans were metropolitan men. We stayed in tents in one riverside village, and visited others. At the village called Providencia we saw a sight which moved us, and which shocked the men.

The first thing we saw when we climbed the riverbank to the village of Providencia was the deer. It was roped to a tree on the grass clearing near the thatch shelter where we would eat lunch.

The deer was small, about the size of a whitetail fawn, but apparently full-grown. It had a rope around its neck and three feet caught in the rope. Someone said that the dogs had caught it that morning and the villagers were going to cook and eat it that night.

This clearing lay at the edge of the little thatched-hut village. We could see the villagers going about their business, scattering feed corn for hens about their houses, and wandering down paths to the river to bathe. The village headman was our host; he stood beside us as we watched the deer struggle. Several village boys were interested in the deer; they formed part of the circle we made around it in the clearing. So also did four businessmen from Quito who were attempting to guide us around the jungle. Few of the very different people standing in this circle had a common language. We watched the deer, and no one said much.

The deer lay on its side at the rope's very end, so the rope lacked slack to let it rest its head in the dust. It was "pretty," delicate of bone like all deer, and thin-skinned for the tropics. Its skin looked virtually hairless, in fact, and almost translucent, like a membrane. Its neck was no thicker than my wrist; it was rubbed open on the rope, and gashed. Trying to paw itself free of the rope, the deer had scratched its own neck with its hooves. The raw underside of its neck showed red stripes and some bruises bleeding inside the muscles. Now three of its feet were hooked in the rope under its jaw. It could not stand, of course, on one leg, so it could not move to slacken the rope and ease the pull on its throat and enable it to rest its head.

Repeatedly the deer paused, motionless, its eyes veiled, with only its rib cage in motion, and its breaths the only sound. Then, after I would think, "It has given up; now it will die," it would heave. The rope twanged; the tree leaves clattered; the deer's free foot beat the ground. We stepped back and held our breaths. It thrashed, kicking, but only one leg moved; the other three legs tightened inside the rope's loop. Its hip jerked; its spine shook. Its eyes rolled; its tongue, thick with spittle, pushed in and out. Then it would rest again. We watched this for fifteen minutes.

Once three young native boys charged in, released its trapped legs, and jumped back to the circle of people. But instantly the deer scratched up its neck with its hooves and snared its forelegs in the rope again. It was easy to imagine a third and then a fourth leg soon stuck, like Brer Rabbit and the Tar Baby.

We watched the deer from the circle, and then we drifted on to lunch. Our palm-roofed shelter stood on a grassy promontory from which we could see the deer tied to the tree, pigs and hens walking under village houses, and black-and-white cattle standing in the river. There was even a breeze.

Lunch, which was the second and better lunch we had that day, was hot and fried. There was a big fish called *doncella*, a kind of catfish, dipped whole in corn flour and beaten egg, then deep fried. With our fingers we pulled soft fragments of it from its sides to our plates, and ate; it was delicate fish-flesh, fresh and mild. Someone found the roe, and I ate of that too—it was fat and stronger, like egg yolk, naturally enough, and warm.

There was also a stew of meat in shreds with rice and pale brown gravy. I had asked what kind of deer it was tied to the tree; Pepe had answered in Spanish, *"Gama."*

Now they told us this was *gama* too, stewed. I suspect the word means merely game or venison. At any rate, I heard that the village dogs had cornered another deer just yesterday, and it was this deer which we were now eating in full sight of the whole article. It was good. I was surprised at its tenderness. But it is a fact that high levels of lactic acid, which builds up in muscle tissues during exertion, tenderizes.

After the fish and meat we ate bananas fried in chunks and served on a tray; they were sweet and full of flavor. I felt terrific. My shirt was wet and cool from swimming; I had had a night's sleep, two decent walks, three meals, and a swim—everything tasted good. From time to time each one of us, separately, would look beyond our shaded roof to the sunny spot where the deer was still convulsing in the dust. Our meal completed, we walked around the deer and back to the boats.

That night I learned that while we were watching the deer, the others were watching me.

We four North Americans grew close in the jungle in a way that was not the usual artificial intimacy of travelers. We liked each other. We stayed up all that night talking, murmuring, as though we rocked on hammocks slung above time. The others were from big cities: New York, Washington, Boston. They all said that I had no expression on my face when I was watching the deer—or at any rate, not the expression they expected.

They had looked to see how I, the only woman, and the youngest, was taking the sight of the deer's struggles. I looked detached, apparently, or hard, or calm, or focused, still. I don't know. I was thinking. I remember feeling very old and energetic. I could say like Thoreau that I have traveled widely in Roanoke, Virginia. I have thought a great deal about carnivorousness; I eat meat. These things are not issues; they are mysteries.

Gentlemen of the city, what surprises you? That there is *suffering* here, or that I know it?

We lay in the tent and talked. "If it had been my wife," one man said with special vigor, amazed, "she wouldn't have cared *what* was going on; she would have dropped *everything* right at that moment and gone in the village from here to there to there, she would not have *stopped* until that animal was out of its suffering one way or another. She couldn't *bear* to see a creature in agony like that."

I nodded.

Now I am home. When I wake I comb my hair before the mirror above my dresser. Every morning for the past two years I have seen in that mirror, beside my sleep-softened face, the blackened face of a burnt man. It is a wire-service photograph clipped from a newspaper and taped to my mirror. The caption reads: "Alan McDonald in Miami hospital bed." All you can see in the photograph is a smudged triangle of face from his eyelids to his lower lip; the rest is bandages. You cannot see the expression in his eyes; the bandages shade them.

The story, headed MAN BURNED FOR SECOND TIME, begins:

"Why does God hate me?" Alan McDonald asked from his hospital bed.

"When the gunpowder went off, I couldn't believe it," he said. "I just couldn't believe it. I said, 'No, God couldn't do this to me again.'"

He was in a burn ward in Miami, in serious condition. I do not even know if he lived. I wrote him a letter at the time, cringing.

He had been burned before, thirteen years previously, by flaming gasoline. For years he had been having his body restored and his face remade in dozens of operations. He had been a boy, and then a burnt boy. He had already been stunned by what could happen, by how life could veer.

Once I read that people who survive bad burns tend to go crazy; they have a very high suicide rate. Medicine cannot ease their pain; drugs just leak away, soaking the sheets, because there is no skin to hold them in. The people just lie there and weep. Later they kill themselves. They had not known, before they were burned, that the world included such suffering, that life could permit them personally such pain.

This time a bowl of gunpowder had exploded on McDonald.

"I didn't realize what had happened at first," he recounted. "And then I heard that sound from 13 years ago. I was burning. I rolled to put the fire out and I thought, 'Oh God, not again.'

"If my friend hadn't been there, I would have jumped into a canal with a rock around my neck."

His wife concludes the piece, "Man, it just isn't fair."

I read the whole clipping again every morning. This is the Big Time here, every minute of it. Will someone please explain to Alan McDonald in his dignity, to the deer at Providencia in his dignity, what is going on? And mail me the carbon.

When we walked by the deer at Providencia for the last time, I said to Pepe, with a pitying glance at the deer, *"Pobrecito"*—"poor little thing." But I was trying out Spanish. I knew at the time it was a ridiculous thing to say.

A Field of Silence

There is a place called "the farm" where I lived once, in a time that was very lonely. Fortunately I was unconscious of my loneliness then, and felt it only deeply, bewildered, in the half-bright way that a puppy feels pain.

I loved the place, and still do. It was an ordinary farm, a calf-raising, haymaking farm, and very beautiful. Its flat, messy pastures ran along one side of the central portion of a quarter-mile road in the central part of an island, an island in Puget Sound, on the Washington coast, so that from the high end of the road you could look west toward the Pacific, to the sound and its hundred islands, and from the other end—and from the farm—you could see east to the water between you and the mainland, and beyond it the mainland's mountains slicked with snow.

I liked the clutter about the place, the way everything blossomed or seeded or rusted; I liked the hundred half-finished projects, the smells, and the way the animals always broke loose. It is calming to herd animals. Often a regular rodeo breaks out—two people and a clever cow can kill a morning—but still, it is calming. You laugh for a while, exhausted, and silence is restored; the beasts are back in their pastures, the fences are not fixed but disguised as if they were fixed, ensuring the animals' temporary resignation; and a great calm descends, a lack of urgency, a sense of having to invent something to do until the next time you must run and chase cattle.

The farm seemed eternal in the crude way the earth does—extending, that is, a very long time. The farm was as old as earth, always there, as old as the island, the Platonic form of "farm," of human society itself, a piece of land eaten and replenished a billion summers, a piece of land worked on, lived on, grown over, plowed under, and stitched again and again, with fingers or with leaves, in and out and into human life's thin weave. I lived there once.

I lived there once and I have seen, from behind the barn, the long roadside pastures heaped with silence. Behind the rooster, suddenly, I saw the silence heaped on the fields like trays. That day the green hayfields supported silence evenly sown; the fields bent just so under the even pressure of silence, bearing it, palming it aloft: cleared fields, part of a land, a planet, that did not buckle beneath the heel of silence, nor split up scattered to bits, but instead lay secret, disguised as time and matter as though that were nothing, ordinary—disguised as fields like those which bear the silence only because they are spread, and the silence spreads over them, great in size.

I do not want, I think, ever to see such a sight again. That there is loneliness here I had granted, in the abstract—but not, I thought, inside the light of God's presence, inside his sanction, and signed by his name.

I lived alone in the farmhouse and rented; the owners, in their twenties, lived in another building just over the yard. I had been reading and restless for two or three days. It was morning. I had just read at breakfast an Updike story, "Packed Dirt, Churchgoing, A Dying Cat, A Traded Car," which moved me. I heard our own farmyard rooster and two or three roosters across the street screeching. I quit the house, hoping at heart to see either of the owners, but immediately to watch our rooster as he crowed.

It was Saturday morning late in the summer, in early September, clear-aired and still. I climbed the barnyard fence between the poultry and the pastures; I watched the red rooster, and the rooster, reptilian, kept one alert and alien eye on me. He pulled his extravagant neck to its maximum length, hauled himself high on his legs, stretched his beak as if he were gagging, screamed, and blinked. It was a ruckus. The din came from everywhere, and only the most rigorous application of reason could persuade me that it proceeded in its entirety from this lone and maniac bird.

After a pause, the roosters across the street started, answering the proclamation, or cranking out another round, arhythmically, interrupting. In the same way there is no pattern nor sense to the massed stridulations of cicadas; their skipped beats, enjambments, and failed alterations jangle your spirits, as though each of those thousand insects, each with identical feelings, were stubbornly deaf to the others, and loudly alone.

I shifted along the fence to see if either of the owners was coming or going. To the rooster I said nothing, but only stared. And he stared at me; we were both careful to keep the wooden fence slat from our line of sight, so that his profiled eye and my two eyes could meet. From time to time I looked beyond the pastures to learn if anyone might be seen on the road.

When I was turned away in this manner, the silence gathered and struck me. It bashed me broadside from the heavens above me like yard goods; ten acres of fallen, invisible sky choked the fields. The pastures on either side of the road turned green in a surrealistic fashion, monstrous, impeccable, as if they were holding their breaths. The roosters stopped. All the things of the world—the fields and the fencing, the road, a parked orange truck—were stricken and self-conscious. A world pressed down on their surfaces, a world battered just within their surfaces, and that real world, so near to emerging, had got stuck.

There was only silence. It was the silence of matter caught in the act and embarrassed. There were no cells moving, and yet there were cells. I could see the shape of the land, how it lay holding silence. Its poise and its stillness were unendurable, like the ring of the silence you hear in your skull when you're little and notice you're living, the ring which resumes later in life when you're sick.

There were flies buzzing over the dirt by the henhouse, moving in circles and buzzing, black dreams in chips off the one long dream, the dream of the regular world. But the silent fields were the real world, eternity's outpost in time, whose look I remembered but never like this, this God-blasted, paralyzed day. I felt myself tall and vertical, in a blue shirt, self-conscious, and wishing to die. I heard the flies again; I looked at the rooster who was frozen looking at me.

Then at last I heard whistling, human whistling far on the air, and I was not able to bear it. I looked around, heartbroken; only at the big yellow Charolais farm far up the road was there motion—a woman, I think, dressed in pink, and pushing a wheelbarrow easily over the grass. It must have been she who was whistling and heaping on top of the silence those hollow notes of song. But the slow sound of the music—the beautiful sound of the music ringing the air like a stone bell—was isolate and detached. The notes spread into the general air and became the weightier part of silence, silence's last straw. The distant woman and her wheelbarrow were flat and detached, like mechanized and pink-painted properties for a stage. I stood in pieces, afraid I was unable to move. Something had unhinged the world. The houses and roadsides and pastures were buckling under the silence. Then a Labrador, black, loped up the distant driveway, fluid and cartoonlike, toward the pink woman. I had to try to turn away. Holiness is a force, and like the others can be resisted. It was given, but I didn't want to see it, God or no God. It was as if God had said, "I am here, but not as you have known me. This is the look of silence, and of loneliness unendurable; it too has always been mine, and now will be yours." I was not ready for a life of sorrow, sorrow deriving from knowledge I could just as well stop at the gate.

I turned away, willful, and the whole show vanished. The realness of things disassembled. The whistling became ordinary, familiar; the air above the fields released its pressure and the fields lay hooded as before. I myself could act. Looking to the rooster I whistled to him myself, softly, and some hens appeared at the chicken house window, greeted the day, and fluttered down.

Several months later, walking past the farm on the way to a volleyball game, I remarked to a friend, by way of information, "There are angels in those fields." Angels! That silence so grave and so stricken, that choked and unbearable green! I have rarely been so surprised at something I've said. Angels! What are angels? I had never thought of angels, in any way at all.

From that time I began to think of angels. I considered that sights such as I had seen of the silence must have been shared by the people who said they saw angels. I began to review the thing I had seen that morning. My impression now of those fields is of thousands of spirits—spirits trapped, perhaps, by my refusal to call them more fully, or by the paralysis of my own spirit at that time—thousands of spirits, angels in fact, almost discernible to the eye, and whirling. If pressed I would say they were three or four feet from the ground. Only their motion was clear (clockwise, if you insist); that, and their beauty unspeakable.

There are angels in those fields, and, I presume, in all fields, and everywhere else. I would go to the lions for this conviction, to witness this fact. What all this means about perception, or language, or angels, or my own sanity, I have no idea.

Guides to Reflection

Deer at Providencia

1. Dillard's fellow travelers are shocked by her response to the deer at Providencia. How do you respond to her description of the sufferings of the deer? Reread the paragraphs in which Dillard tells of watching the deer and eating her lunch. What do her feelings about the deer and the food seem to be? Look for particular words that reveal her feelings. Review also her comments about the burned man. Why do you think she keeps his picture on her bedroom mirror at home?

2. The deer at Providencia falls victim to the workings of nature's food chain (an "ordinary" event), and the man in Florida suffers two sudden disasters ("extraordinary" events). Why might Dillard set these two kinds

of suffering beside each other in the essay? How do they relate to each other?

3. Dillard five times names the Ecuadorian village where she sees the deer: in the title, twice at the beginning of the essay, and twice at the end. Traditionally, *Providence* is a word Christians have used to name the goodness of God; the term *divine providence* expresses the Christian belief that God has a plan for creation, one that moves it toward a good end. How does Dillard present God in this essay? Is Providence apparent? Why or why not?

A Field of Silence

1. Dillard uses strong language to describe her experience in the field. She says, for instance, that "the silence gathered and *struck* me. It *bashed* me broadside . . ." (editor's emphasis). Reread the essay looking for other examples of this kind of language. Why might Dillard use language like this? What kind of effect does it have on you? How does it affect your impression of and response to her experience?

2. How does Dillard react to the voice of God and the presence of angels in the field? Consider how her immediate response differs from her later ones, when she talks with her friend and then writes this essay. What picture of God does Dillard present in the essay?

3. Where have you been most likely to listen for and discover the "sacred or holy"?

Alice Walker

At the end of Alice Walker's latest novel, *Possessing the Secret of Joy* (1992), a character being led off to her death sees the huge block letters of a sign held up by one of her friends. It reads, "Resistance is the secret of joy." Throughout her five novels, two collections of essays, and several books of poetry, Walker has understood resistance as more than a matter of survival; for her it is also an article of faith. Writing as a Black who is also a "womanist," she is concerned as much with gender as with race: "I am preoccupied with the spiritual survival, the survival *whole* of my people. But beyond that, I am committed to exploring the oppressions, the insanities, the loyalties, and the triumphs of black women."[1] For her, resistance means refusing to die, to be mutilated in body or soul, to lose faith in the divine spirit with whom we are all meant to be "in conspiracy." It also means acting on behalf of others as well as for oneself. Indeed, resistance understood as the solidarity of love is the motivating force behind so much of Walker's work. As she has written in her 1988 collection of essays, *Living by the Word*, "There is no story more moving to me personally than one in which one woman saves the life of another, and saves herself, and slays whatever dragon has appeared."[2]

It is precisely this double salvation, of another person and of oneself, that Walker portrayed in her most remarkable work to date, *The Color Purple* (1982).[3] It is also here that her explicitly theological preoccupations surface most clearly. As the author writes in her preface to the tenth anniversary edition, her intent in telling Celie's story was "to explore the difficult path of someone who starts in life already a spiritual captive, but who, through her own courage and the help of others," discovers herself to be an expression of the divine.[4] Celie's movement from the religious to the spiritual—from traditional Christianity to something like pantheism ("I believe God is everything")—also describes Walker's own journey. While retaining an admiration for the person of Christ, she acknowledges herself drawn to a God who cannot be represented by race or gender. Therefore she prefers to speak of "The Great Mystery," or of "All That Is, " or of "That Which Is Beyond Understanding But Not Beyond Loving." As Shug says in *The Color Purple*, "God is inside you and inside everybody else."[5]

Increasingly for Walker, God is also inside nature. She feels the Spirit "moving in beauty across the grassy hills" rather than in the words of Sunday sermons "or through any human mouth."[6] It would be a mistake, however, to underestimate Walker's connection to history, to the religious experience of African Americans, and to the specific heritage of resistance that is both black and Christian. A case in point is "The Welcome Table," a short story that appeared in her 1973 collection, *In Love and Trouble: Stories of Black Women.*[7] The collection as a whole explores the failure of women either to save one another or themselves. Most of these characters find themselves in love and therefore in trouble, helpless to rise up against the forces of racism and misogyny that threaten to destroy them. One of the stories that proves the exception to this rule is "The Welcome Table," which takes its name from the spiritual that serves as its epigraph and is dedicated to the gospel singer "sister Clara Ward." Even before the opening line of her story, therefore, Walker indicates the context in which she wants it to be read. She invokes an ancestry of resistance, a sisterhood of black "foremothers" who kept the race alive. Likewise, she foregrounds the importance of spirituals, reminding us of that great musical tradition that empowered blacks first to resist slavery and then to survive its ongoing consequences. No doubt Walker also had in mind the role of spirituals in the work of Harriet Tubman, who used these songs of faith to lead masses of runaway slaves to their freedom. She may also have been thinking of one of her personal role models, Sojourner Truth, who composed songs to be sung at abolitionist meetings in order to get people "moving" against injustice: "I am pleading for my people, / A poor downtrodden race, / Who dwell in freedom's boasted land, / With no abiding place."[8]

In this story, Walker brings an old woman to church, to that "welcome table" where Christians are called to worship. Although wretchedly poor, she is wearing her best "Sunday-go-to-meeting clothes"; although ancient, she has staggered down a country road half a mile from her house, drawn by the glittering cross that crowns the church's steeple and by the desire to come to the Welcome Table on the Lord's day. What makes this simple act inadmissible is that, forgetful and nearly blind with age, she has come to the *wrong* church. Oblivious to the color barrier that divides her entire culture, she breaks a boundary and thereby destroys the peace. The minister reminds "Auntie" at the door that this is not her place; an usher tells "Grandma" that she must leave; but finally it is the ladies of the church who make their men do their duty to God and country by picking her up and throwing her out.

What is the threat she poses? The story raises all the possibilities: she is old, black, and "different"; she represents the possibility of a servant class stepping out of line; she is the mother of African orgy and urban anarchy; she is the desecration of *their* Holy Church. With her "aged blue-brown eyes," she is also, no doubt, a reminder of the intermingling of their own blood with hers, a mixture of race that is also a history of rape.

From her entrance into the church right up until her forced exit, the old woman is engaged in the single form of resistance still within her power: "She had been singing in her head. They had interrupted her. Promptly she began to sing again" (p. 112). Made unwelcome at the church's Welcome Table, she is nonetheless free (in the words of the spiritual cited as in the epigraph) to "Shout my troubles over / Walk and talk with Jesus." Suddenly the spiritual's metaphor takes on the aspect of a dream or a hallucination, as the Jesus who "walks" with Christians on their way to Zion appears to her in the highway across from the church. He looks exactly like the Tender Shepherd familiar to her from the picture hanging over her bed at home, a Caucasian savior stolen from "a white lady's Bible." Yet, if white, he is no more at home in the church than is the old woman herself. And it is to her and not to them that he says, as to his disciples, "Follow me." And so she does, singing out loud "some of the old spirituals she loved," and walking with Jesus toward a destination at once wonderful and unknown.

For Alice Walker, the old woman incarnates the power of the black spiritual, its determination to "cross over Jordan" no matter what. Indeed, it might be argued that among the thirteen women of *In Love and Trouble*—Walker elsewhere calls them "mad, raging, loving, resentful, hateful, strong, ugly, weak, pitiful, and magnificent"[9]—it is this ancient lady with her withered corsage and greasy headrag who is the real heroine of the collection. For it is she who throws off oppression by keeping her song and her faith alive, she whose walk with God is her most profound act of resistance.

Peter S. Hawkins

Notes

1. Alice Walker, *In Search of Our Mothers' Gardens* (San Diego: Harcourt Brace Jovanovich, 1983), 250.

2. Alice Walker, *Living By the Word* (San Diego: Harcourt Brace Jovanovich, 1988), 19.

3. Alice Walker, *The Color Purple* (San Diego: Harcourt Brace Jovanovich, 1982).

4. *The Color Purple* (San Diego: Harcourt Brace Jovanovich, 1992), xi.

5. *The Color Purple*, 177.

6. *The Color Purple* (1992), xi.

7. Alice Walker, *In Love and Trouble: Stories of Black Women* (San Diego: Harcourt Brace Jovanovich, 1973).

8. Cited in *Journey Toward Freedom: The Story of Sojourner Truth*, ed. Jacqueline Bernard (New York: Feminist Press, distributed by Talman Company, 1990), 149-150.

9. *In Search of Our Mothers' Gardens*, 251.

The Welcome Table

for sister Clara Ward

I'm going to sit at the Welcome table
Shout my troubles over
Walk and talk with Jesus
Tell God how you treat me
One of these days!

—*Spiritual*

The old woman stood with eyes uplifted in her Sunday-go-to-meeting clothes: high shoes polished about the tops and toes, a long rusty dress adorned with an old corsage, long withered, and the remnants of an elegant silk scarf as headrag stained with grease from the many oily pigtails underneath. Perhaps she had known suffering. There was a dazed and sleepy look in her aged blue-brown eyes. But for those who searched hastily for "reasons" in that old tight face, shut now like an ancient door, there was nothing to be read. And so they gazed nakedly upon their own fear transferred; a fear of the black and the old, a terror of the unknown as well as of the deeply known. Some of those who saw her there on the church steps spoke words about her that were hardly fit to be heard, others held their pious peace; and some felt vague stirrings of pity, small and persistent and hazy, as if she were an old collie turned out to die.

She was angular and lean and the color of poor gray Georgia earth, beaten by king cotton and the extreme weather. Her elbows were wrinkled and thick, the skin ashen but durable, like the bark of old pines. On her face centuries were folded into the circles around one eye, while around the other, etched and mapped as if for print, ages more threatened again to live. Some of them there at the church saw the age, the dotage, the missing buttons down the front of her mildewed black dress. Others saw cooks, chauffeurs, maids, mistresses, children denied or smothered in the deferential way she held her cheek to the side, toward the ground. Many of them saw jungle orgies in an evil place, while others were reminded of riotous anarchists looting and raping in the streets. Those who knew the hesitant creeping up on them of the law, saw the beginning of the end of the sanctuary of Christian worship, saw the desecration of Holy Church, and saw an invasion of privacy, which they struggled to believe they still kept.

Still she had come down the road toward the big white church alone. Just herself, an old forgetful woman, nearly blind with age. Just her and her eyes raised dully to the glittering cross that crowned the sheer silver steeple. She had walked along the road in a stagger from her house a half mile away. Perspiration, cold and clammy, stood on her brow and along the creases by her thin wasted nose. She stopped to calm herself on the wide front steps, not looking about her as they might have expected her to do, but simply standing quite still, except for a slight quivering of her throat and tremors that shook her cotton-stockinged legs.

The reverend of the church stopped her pleasantly as she stepped into the vestibule. Did he say, as they thought he did, kindly, "Auntie, you know this is not your church?" As if one could choose the wrong one. But no one remembers, for they never spoke of it afterward, and she brushed past him anyway, as if she had been brushing past him all her life, except this time she was in a hurry. Inside the church she sat on the very first bench from the back, gazing with concentration at the stained-glass window over her head. It was cold, even inside the church, and she was shivering. Everybody could see. They stared at her as they came in and sat down near the front. It was cold, very cold to them, too; outside the church it was below freezing and not much above inside. But the sight of her, sitting there somehow passionately ignoring them, brought them up short, burning.

The young usher, never having turned anyone out of his church before, but not even considering this job as *that* (after all, she had no right to be there, certainly), went up to her and whispered that she should leave. Did he call her "Grandma," as later he seemed to recall he had? But for those who actually hear such traditional pleasantries and to whom they actually mean something, "Grandma" was not one, for she did not pay him any attention, just muttered, "Go 'way," in a weak sharp *bothered* voice, waving his frozen blond hair and eyes from near her face.

It was the ladies who finally did what to them had to be done. Daring their burly indecisive husbands to throw the old colored woman out they made their point. God, mother, country, earth, church. It involved all that, and well they knew it. Leather bagged and shoed, with good calfskin gloves to keep out the cold, they looked with contempt at the bloodless gray arthritic hands of the old woman, clenched loosely, restlessly in her lap.

Could their husbands expect them to sit up in church with that? No, no, the husbands were quick to answer and even quicker to do their duty.

Under the old woman's arms they placed their hard fists (which afterward smelled of decay and musk—the fermenting scent of onionskins and rotting greens). Under the old woman's arms they raised their fists, flexed their muscular shoulders, and out she flew through the door, back under the cold blue sky. This done, the wives folded their healthy arms across their trim middles and felt at once justified and scornful. But none of them said so, for none of them ever spoke of the incident again. Inside the church it was warmer. They sang, they prayed. The protection and promise of God's impartial love grew more not less desirable as the sermon gathered fury and lashed itself out above their penitent heads.

The old woman stood at the top of the steps looking about in bewilderment. She had been singing in her head. They had interrupted her. Promptly she began to sing again, though this time a sad song. Suddenly, however, she looked down the long gray highway and saw something interesting and delightful coming. She started to grin, toothlessly, with short giggles of joy, jumping about and slapping her hands on her knees. And soon it became apparent why she was so happy. For coming down the highway at a firm though leisurely pace was Jesus. He was wearing an immaculate white, long dress trimmed in gold around the neck and hem, and a red, a bright red, cape. Over his left arm he carried a brilliant blue blanket. He was wearing sandals and a beard and he had long brown hair parted on the right side. His eyes, brown, had wrinkles around them as if he smiled or looked at the sun a lot. She would have known him, recognized him, anywhere. There was a sad but joyful look to his face, like a candle was glowing behind it, and he walked with sure even steps in her direction, as if he were walking on the sea. Except that he was not carrying in his arms a baby sheep, he looked exactly like the picture of him that she had hanging over her bed at home. She had taken it out of a white lady's Bible while she was working for her. She had looked at that picture for more years than she could remember, but never once had she really expected to see him. She squinted her eyes to be sure he wasn't carrying a little sheep in one arm, but he was not. Ecstatically she began to wave her arms for fear he would miss seeing her, for he walked looking straight ahead on the shoulder of the highway, and from time to time looking upward at the sky.

All he said when he got up close to her was "Follow me," and she bounded down to his side with all the bob and speed of one so old. For every one of his long determined steps she made two quick ones. They walked along in deep silence for a long time. Finally she started telling him about how many years she had cooked for them, cleaned for them, nursed them. He looked at her kindly but in silence. She told him indignantly about how they had grabbed her when she was singing in her head and not looking, and how they had tossed her out of his church. A old heifer like me, she said, straightening up next to Jesus, breathing hard. But he smiled down at her and she felt better instantly and time just seemed to fly by. When they passed her house, forlorn and sagging, weatherbeaten and patched, by the side of the road, she did not even notice it, she was so happy to be out walking along the highway with Jesus.

She broke the silence once more to tell Jesus how glad she was that he had come, how she had often looked at his picture hanging on her wall (she hoped he didn't know she had stolen it) over her bed, and how she had never expected to see him down here in person. Jesus gave her one of his beautiful smiles and they walked on. She did not know where they were going; someplace wonderful, she suspected. The ground was like clouds under their feet, and she felt she could walk forever without becoming the least bit tired. She even began to sing out loud some of the old spirituals she loved, but she didn't want to annoy Jesus, who looked so thoughtful, so she quieted down. They walked on, looking straight over the treetops into the sky, and the smiles that played over her dry wind-cracked face were like first clean ripples across a stagnant pond. On they walked without stopping.

The people in church never knew what happened to the old woman; they never mentioned her to one another or to anybody else. Most of them heard sometime later that an old colored woman fell dead along the highway. Silly as it seemed, it appeared she had walked herself to death. Many of the black families along the road said they had seen the old lady high-stepping down the highway; sometimes jabbering in a low insistent voice, sometimes singing, sometimes merely gesturing excitedly with her hands. Other times silent and smiling, looking at the sky. She had been alone, they said. Some of them wondered aloud where the old woman had been going so stoutly that it had worn her heart out. They guessed maybe she had relatives across the river, some miles away, but none of them really knew.

Guides to Reflection

1. Given her age, fragility, and general disorientation, the old woman who comes to church in her "Sunday-go-to-meeting clothes" would seem

to offer no more than an embarrassment, and one that might most easily simply be ignored. Yet this is precisely what cannot be allowed. Discuss the several reasons given by the author to explain why the church people find this doddering old woman to be such a threat. If "racism" is the cause, name the fears that contribute toward it.

2. The old woman recognizes the man walking down the highway as Jesus because he resembles exactly the picture of the Tender Shepherd she had looked at for years but had never expected actually to see in the flesh. What point is Walker trying to make when she describes the old woman thinking of Christ as Caucasian because she has received him from a "white lady's Bible"? This suggests how Christianity has been represented to Blacks as a "white" religion that belongs, first and foremost, to the people gathered in the "big white church." In "The Welcome Table," however, Jesus doesn't enter that congregation or say "Follow me" to any of them; instead, he relates exclusively to the old woman. Discuss the relationship between them. What does she ask of him; what does he give?

3. In this story, Walker cultivates an atmosphere more surrealistic than realistic. It is unclear exactly who did what during the time that the old woman was in the church; what eventually happens on the highway, as she and Jesus "walked without stopping," is also highly mysterious. What is the effect of this cultivation of uncertainty? To what degree is it important to determine what is meant to be happening and what is only conjecture? Why? Is this Walker's way of dealing with "visionary" material?

4. Read James 2:1-5. What connections, if any, do you see between this portion of "biblical wisdom" and the story? Think about your own congregation. Is it a place where "misfits" are welcome? What makes a "misfit" anyway?

Garrison Keillor

Garrison Keillor has become well known as a storyteller on his public radio programs. Over the past twenty years, Keillor has attracted a large audience for his shows, which revolve around his monologues and have a homey, midwestern tone. Yet, at the same time, he has also had distinctly different, more "literary" stories published in the *New Yorker* and the *Atlantic Monthly*, magazines with narrower audiences, known for their sophistication, urbanity, and erudition. And his novel and collections of stories have been widely and favorably reviewed. Keillor's abilities to write well in a variety of genres and to appeal to various audiences are striking and rare.

Keillor's signature piece, the most important of his genres, is the radio monologue. The term "monologue" comes from the drama, and it implies a context for the piece; it makes it part of a play or a show. Keillor's monologues are short stories written expressly for oral rendition during the third half hour of a two-hour radio show. They are, he says, "written for [his] voice, which is flat and slow."[1] On the show, the monologues are surrounded by singing, chatting, and radio theater.

In the monologues on "A Prairie Home Companion," his show from 1974–87, Keillor tells stories of people living in Lake Wobegon, Minnesota, a town that both time and cartographers have forgotten, a town seemingly much like Keillor's actual hometown, Anoka, Minnesota. The monologues always begin "It's been a quiet week in Lake Wobegon, my hometown." And they always end "And that's the news from Lake Wobegon, where all the women are strong, all the men are good-looking, and all the children are above average." Within this framework, Keillor weaves stories with a large but recurring cast of characters, using particular situations and themes to give the monologues coherence.

Keillor often introduces religion as one of the monologues' organizing themes, and he treats it, like his other themes, humorously. Keillor's humor depends upon his presentation of his characters and arises from the contrasting viewpoints he creates for the stories: the characters', his own, and his audience's. The discrepancies among the viewpoints make the audience laugh, but only because Keillor has drawn us close enough to his characters so that we can see and understand their perspective and feel sympathy for it. Often, out of the laughter, comes an insight for the audience; we understand something not only about Lake Wobegon, but also about ourselves that we had not known or that we had forgotten.

In "Exiles," Keillor tells of city people coming to visit relatives in Lake Wobegon at Christmas. They are looking for reassurance and quiet calm, but on the radio stations and in the living rooms, bedrooms, hallways, and churches of Lake Wobegon, they find or remember something else. The sermons in particular are disturbing. Corinne Ingqvist, for instance, speeds into town at seventy-five mph, "arguing with a preacher on the radio, telling him his theology was repressive." Keillor remembers hiding a radio in his bed at night and happening upon the "Brother Carl and His Wall of Hope Revival Show," hearing what seems to have been an old-fashioned, fire-and-brimstone sermon. Father Emil, ill with cancer, preaches a "hard homily" on Christmas Eve, "inspired by the sight of all the lapsed Catholics parading into church with their unbaptized children." Even dull sermons can be disquieting—Keillor remembers that one exile was "saved twelve times in the Lutheran church, an all-time record"; at least one time his dramatic repentance was in response to a "dry sermon about stewardship."

The listeners to these sermons all want to feel safe, to make the "right" choices in their lives so that the hard things the preachers in their various ways talk about will not hurt them. They want to feel that they have come to the "Y" in the road that Robert Frost describes in his famous poem and that they have made a good choice.

But Lake Wobegon does not offer reassurance on this matter easily. The sermons probably evoke smiles in Keillor's audience; they seem naive, simple-minded. But they also, however oddly, seem to speak to the situations the listeners—native Lake Wobegoners and city dwellers alike—find themselves in. They reveal the unexpected unsettledness of Christmas—something one of the preachers, David Ingqvist, discovers when, as he is in the midst of an argument with his wife, his doorbell rings and a holy family of sorts—his aunt, uncle, and cousin Corinne—are standing outside, uninvited, hoping to be asked in for Christmas dinner.

Things are unexpectedly unsettled in Keillor's story "Aprille" as well. Just before her confirmation at Lake Wobegon Lutheran Church, fourteen-year-old Lois Tollerud decides she may have lost her faith. As she ponders her crisis, the rituals of small town confirmation celebrations proceed. At dinner, Lois's mother presents an elaborately decorated cake; she had used "the extra-fine nozzle on the frosting gun" to write on it, in blue, Lois's confirmation verse from Romans: "Be not conformed to this world: but be ye transformed. . . ."

The many transformations in this story seem to be more complete and somewhat different than any one expected, and the characters are scared by that. Lois loses her faith watching a TV news report on a war in a faraway land, frightened to imagine it coming to Lake Wobegon. The other confirmands, glibly repeating pat, memorized answers to "questions that have troubled theologians for years," are scared, of course, to speak in front of so many people, but they also are sobered to realize that this ceremony marks the beginning of adulthood for them. Keillor tells a story of riding a bus to Minneapolis with his aunt, pretending not to know her, striking up a conversation with her, and then being scared when she pretends not to know him. Eventually, Keillor says, we all change in ways that make us unrecognizable to those who have known or loved us, and that may leave us frightened and adrift.

What then of the transformation St. Paul calls for in Romans? The everyday experiences of transformation in the characters' lives would make one leery of such complete change. But Keillor frames "Aprille" with descriptions of spring; the same beautiful spring comes to Lake Wobegon every year as came to Chaucer's England in "Aprille" 600 years ago. The return of spring suggests constancy even in the midst of change. The end of Lois's verse from Romans promises that as the result of transformation she will find the will of God, which is "good, and acceptable, and perfect." And to close "Aprille," Keillor alludes to Jesus' promise in Matthew that God watches even each sparrow, "and so much more does He watch us all." Transformations in "Aprille" occur within this larger framework, one not always apparent to the characters.

In "Exiles" and "Aprille," Keillor evokes with compelling force the everyday lives of people in his imagined town, Lake Wobegon. In these, as in all his monologues, he presents his characters' experiences, dilemmas, and thoughts with sympathy and gentle irony. These powerfully engaging and extraordinarily popular stories often lead their audience to ponder their own religious beliefs, to reexamine their religious values in light of the experiences of some seemingly unexceptional people living in obscurity in rural Minnesota.

Paula J. Carlson

Notes

1. Garrison Keillor, *Leaving Home* (New York: Viking Penguin Inc., 1987), xvi.

Exiles

It has been a quiet week in Lake Wobegon. Warm and foggy on Tuesday, and late in the day, as the temperature fell, fog froze on the trees and made white bare trees in which the fog appeared ghostly beautiful, as if you could walk into these trees and receive immortal powers of a sort we all want at Christmas: the power to gather our friends and loved ones close around us and prevent suffering and evil and death from touching them.

When I was little, I worried about a group of men I called the Murderers, who had killed before and would kill again because killing meant nothing to them, they had nothing to lose, it was the electric chair for them either way. They were now driving in a stolen black sedan toward a Y in the road where two roads diverged, and if they chose one they'd come to our house and kill us, and if they didn't they wouldn't. I could keep my family safe by prayer. At night I crawled into bed between cold sheets like sheets of ice and prayed for God to keep the Murderers away from us, and as an extra precaution, in addition to prayer, I always got into bed from the left side. I lay on my right side. I prayed the exact same prayer. And although I knew I shouldn't, in the dark I made the sign of the cross, on the odd chance that God was not Protestant. I pulled the blankets up and lay warming my little hollow, listening to the house creak, smelling the Vicks my mother put on me as a precaution, and felt I had kept the Murderers from our door. Then, one night, I got into bed from the wrong side, exposing my family to evil because I was in a hurry, so I got out and got back in on the correct side. But was still afraid. So I took my radio into bed with me. It was the size of a breadbox. I pulled the covers over my head and tuned in Bob Franklin, host of "Music by Moonlight"—the "Old Smoothie," he was called, because he made you feel like you and him were close ("Hello, friends, Bob Franklin here—say, I believe that I know you well enough to say that you're discriminating when it comes to the finer things and particular about the details being just right, just the way you want them, and that's why I know that Jirasek's Dry Cleaning in Albany is just the place for you . . ."). It thrilled me as a boy to hear a man take me into his confidence that way, but instead of old Bob playing Glenn Miller, there was a preacher on the air who wasn't friendly at all and didn't think I was discriminating and didn't think dry cleaning would do me much good one way or the other. He seemed to suggest that the Murderers were standing over my bed about to stab me with an ice pick and that it was exactly what I deserved. What was "Brother Carl and His Wall of Hope Revival Show" doing in place of old Bob and "Music by Moonlite"? Then I checked my clock: it was five-thirty in the morning. We were safe for another day.

Corinne Ingqvist came home for Christmas on Sunday. She came barreling north in her red VW from Minneapolis, arguing with a preacher on the radio, telling him his theology was repressive, when she noticed she was going seventy-five mph. She cruised through the lights of town and turned down the long-familiar driveway to their house by the lake. In the backseat were two tins of tea for gifts and 132 critical essays by her seventeen-year-old students on Robert Frost's poem "The Road Not Taken" ("Two roads diverged in a yellow wood, . . . and I—I took the one less traveled by, And that has made all the difference") that she was planning to grade on Monday. Her parents' house seemed like a quiet retreat with only her and Hjalmar and Virginia for Christmas.

She pulled up the driveway and parked by the old limestone wall. She got out the shopping bag of presents and essays and walked up three steps to the back door and put her bare hand on the cold brass knob and a sudden cold thought came to mind: *This soon shall pass. And it won't be too long.* She swayed slightly and then went in. "Hello," said Hjalmar, and kissed her. "Hello, dear, you look so wonderful," said Virginia. The tree in the same place, beside the old piano, in front of the bright fish tank. Orange and silver guppies seemed to swim among the ornaments, drifting to and fro, like orange and silver snowflakes that never reach the ground, fish in the branches among the lights.

Dozens of exiles returned for Christmas. At Our Lady of Perpetual Responsibility, Father Emil roused himself from bed, where he's been down with cancer since Columbus Day, and said Christmas Eve Mass. He was inspired by the sight of all the lapsed Catholics parading into church with their unbaptized children, and he gave them a hard homily, strolling right down into the congregation. "Shame. Shame on us for leaving what we were given that was true and good," he said. "To receive a great treasure in our younger days and to abandon it so that we can lie down in the mud with swine." He stood, one hand on the back of a pew, and everyone in that pew—children of this church who grew up and moved away and did well and now tell humorous stories at parties about Father Emil and what it was like to grow up Catholic—all of them shuddered a little, afraid he might grab them by their Harris-tweed collars and stand them up and ask them questions. "What a shame. What a shame." They came for Christmas, to hear music and see the candles and smell incense and feel hopeful, and here was their old priest with hair in his ears whacking them around—was it a brain cancer he had? *Shame, shame on us.* He looked around at all the little children he'd given first communion to, now grown heavy and prosperous and sad and indolent, but clever enough to explain their indolence and sadness as a rebellion against orthodoxy, a protest, adventurous, intellectual, which really was only dullness of spirit. He stopped. It was so quiet you could hear them not breathing. Then he said that this was why Our Lord had come, to rescue us from dullness of spirit, and so the shepherds had found and so shall we, and then it was Christmas again.

Dozens of exiles were back, including some whom their families weren't expecting because they'd said they weren't coming, couldn't come, were sorry but it was just out of the question. But Christmas exerts powerful forces. We turn a corner in a wretched shopping mall and some few bars of a tune turn a switch in our heads and gates open and tons of water thunder through Hoover Dam, the big turbines spin, electricity flows, and we get in our car and go back, like salmon.

Larry the Sad Boy was there, who was saved twelve times in the Lutheran church, an all-time record. Between 1953 and 1961, he threw himself weeping and contrite on God's throne of grace on twelve separate occasions—and this in a Lutheran church that wasn't evangelical, had no altar call, no organist playing "Just As I Am Without One Plea" while a choir hummed and a guy with shiny hair took hold of your heartstrings and played you like a cheap guitar—this is the Lutheran church, not a bunch of hillbillies—these are Scandinavians, and they repent in the same way that they sin: discreetly, tastefully, at the proper time, and bring a Jell-O salad for afterward. Larry Sorenson came forward weeping buckets and crumpled up at the communion rail, to the amazement of the minister, who had delivered a dry sermon about stewardship, and who now had to put his arm around this limp soggy individual and pray with him and see if he had a ride home. *Twelve times.* Even we fundamentalists got tired of him. Granted, we're born in original sin and are worthless and vile, but twelve conversions is too many. God didn't mean us to feel guilt all our lives. There comes a point when you should dry your tears and join the building committee and start grappling with the problems of the church furnace and the church roof and make church coffee and be of use, but Larry kept on repenting and repenting. He came up for Christmas and got drunk and knocked over the Christmas tree. That was before 2:00 P.M. He spent the next eight hours apologizing for it, and the penance was worse than the crime.

Eddie the Jealous Boy came home. He told his parents that he wasn't going to come, but they didn't protest enough, and he felt unwanted and so he came up with his lovely wife, Eunice. She is the most beautiful woman ever to leave Lake Wobegon, having been elected Tri-County Queen in 1960, Miss Sixth Congressional District the same year, first runner-up in the 1962 Miss Midwest contest, and then Miss Upper Mississippi Basin by the U.S. Corps of Engineers, and having won them all, she retired from royalty because it made Eddie crazy to see other men look at her and like her. If she so much as touched a man on the arm in a friendly way, it meant she'd later spend hours listening to Eddie's hot dry angry voice and endure days of his silence, and so this funny and lovely woman has tried to please him and make herself quiet and dull and unattractive, but he's more jealous than ever. On Christmas afternoon, when he looked up from a robot he was assembling and noticed that Eunice and her brother-in-law Fred were nowhere to be seen, he tore around in a frenzy, ran outdoors, got in the car (there is no motel in town), and headed for the skating rink. The warming house was open. Maybe they were kissing in there. Maybe they were skating together. Maybe they were off in the woods, naked in the snow. He saw her alone, walking. He jumped out, ran up, and said, "Where is he? Where's Fred?" She stared back at him with a dull look in her eyes. "Fred didn't come for Christmas this year," she said. "Don't you remember? He and Marcie went to Des Moines."

Corinne put off grading those papers until Monday and got busy baking cookies and some little currant buns from an old Norwegian recipe. She hadn't had them since she was little, and now she was baking them herself. Amazing: a delicious smell from childhood that brings back every sweet old aunt and grandma as if they're there beside you, and you do it with just a little saffron. Monday night she made herself start those papers, and then carolers came, and it wasn't until Tuesday afternoon that she really faced up to it, 132 essays of five hundred words each, about seventy thousand words about the poem "Two roads diverged in a yellow wood, . . . and I—I took the one less traveled by, And that has made all the difference." And of those words at least ten thousand were *I, me,* or *mine—This poem makes me think of what happened to me when I was ten and my parents said to me.* . . . For them, all roads converged into the first person singular. It was hard reading, very hard, and their teacher finally chose the road that led away from the stack of essays toward the Christmas tree and the fish tank. A lovely thing about Christmas is that it's compulsory, like a thunderstorm, and we all go through it together, it's not individual, it's sociable.

Foxy the Proud Boy came home, but now he is Richard to everyone, except among his close pals in the grain-futures business in Minneapolis, where he is Pinky. He drove up in a pink 1987 Ferlinghetti, a car so fabulous that when he sits in it, even en route to his origins in a little house painted lavatory green, he feels attractive and *special*. He forgets his dull seedy relatives, who come out and look at his fantastic car, its red leather seats, the incredible instrument panel that shows you the tides, the movements of planets and galaxies. They peer in the tinted windows and say, "Cheess, there's no room in there, Richard—two seats—what are you thinking of— whaddaya do when you got things to haul?" They don't see that Richard is traveling light, he's secure in himself, and with Vanessa sitting next to him, that's a total reality and his life is complete, and yet—Why does he turn pale when he leads this fabulous woman in a silver-lamé shirt into the dim little house? Why does he tremble? Is it the pictures on the walls: the praying hands, the *Threshers* by Millet, a Winslow Homer ship, nee- dlepoint, "Ve Get Too Soon Oldt and Too Late Schmardt"? Is it his family, who never learned the art of making conversation because they only talk to people they know? A slow and terrible death, asphyxiation in your own past. All afternoon he's dying to get back in the Ferlinghetti and go home. At the first decent opportunity, he begins the long ritual good-bye: Well, I guess it's time we . . . No, really, Ma. Vanessa has to (lie lie lie). Well, okay, just one, but then we got to (lie). No, I'd like to but we promised these friends we'd (lie lie). Finally, with a wave and a roar, they pull away and she turns to Richard the Proud and says, "They were nice. I liked them." But his eyes are full of tears, from exhaustion and relief and guilt and from pride—he really does love this car, it gives him so much pleasure.

Corinne didn't see Richard, Larry, or Eddie. She stayed home. On Christmas Eve, she and Hjalmar and Virginia sat and talked and listened to the Mormon Tabernacle Choir, both sides, A and B, and their old scratchy record of Lionel Barrymore in *A Christmas Carol*. They watched Midnight Mass from Saint Patrick's Cathedral in New York and ate the saffron buns. In the morning, Hjalmar took their dog, Puddles, for a walk. A mile away, the old dog was exhausted. Hjalmar had to pick him up and carry him home. Hjalmar was too tired to drive into Saint Cloud to the Powers Hotel for the elegant Christmas buffet, and so, because there were only three of them, Corinne said, "Let's not fuss, let's make a little turkey dinner with the microwave Daddy got you for Christmas last year." "Fine," Virginia said, "it's under the bed in the guest room, in the box." They both studied the operating manual. In its attempt to describe the incredible flexibility of the microwave, its various functions and options and alter- natives, the infinite variety and joy of the thing, it bewildered them. The control panel had buttons numbered from 0 to 9 and other buttons that said: Over, Stop, Clear, From, Time, Recall, Auto, Memory. Which brought back the memory of how lovely it was to put water in a pot, boil it, and drop stuff in—"No!" Corinne cried. "We can't let electronics defeat us!" They put the frozen turkey-dinner pouches in the microwave, pushed a combination of buttons that made the light go on and the fan whirr, and left the kitchen and went and conversed until the bell rang, but something was wrong: the peas were a bluish green, the pouch of turkey had flecks of silvery ash in it. They had each had two glasses of sherry and were in a philosophical mood. Corinne looked at her mother, her mother looked at Corinne. "Well," said Corinne, "I'll never have babies." "So," said Virginia, "I'll never be a grandma." "That's life," they said, "let's go to David and Judy's and see what Christian charity really is worth nowadays. They invited us, didn't they—? It was a month ago and we said no, but we didn't know then what we know now, so let's go."

The Reverend David Ingqvist and wife, Judith, were in the midst of an argument when they heard the knock on the door. They were arguing whether she is always wrong or not: she was saying that, yes, she can never do any thing right and never pleases him, and he was saying that, no, she was wrong now but she is usually right and, no, she often pleases him and, yes, he does tell her—when he opened the door, expecting to find someone with a gift in hand, and saw his aunt and uncle and cousin. "Hello," said Hjalmar. "We thought we'd come down." "How are you?" said Virginia. "Merry Christmas." "What're you having for dinner?" asked Corinne. "Aren't you going to invite us in?"

Aprille

It has been a quiet week in Lake Wobegon. Spring has come, grass is green, the trees are leafing out, birds arriving every day by the busload, and now the Norwegian bachelor farmers are washing their sheets. In town the windows are open, so, as you pause in your walk to admire Mrs. Hoglund's rock garden, you can smell her floor wax and hear the piano lesson she is giving, the tune that goes "da da Da da Da da da," and up by school, smell the macaroni cheese hotdish for lunch and hear from upstairs the voices of Miss Melrose's class reciting Chaucer.

> Whan that Aprille with his shoures soote
> The droghte of March hath perced to the roote
> And bathed every veyne in swich licour
> Of which vertu engendred is the flour;
> Whan Zephyrus eek with his sweete breeth
> Inspired hath in every holt and heeth
> The tendre croppes, and the yonge sonne
> Hath in the Ram his halve cours yronne
> And smale fowles maken melodye
> That slepen al the nyght with open ye . . .

The words are six hundred years old and describe spring in this little town quite well; the sweet breath of the wind, the youth of the sun, the sweet rain, the tendre croppes, the smale fowles maken melodys: we have them all.

I made a pilgrimage up there last Sunday to visit my family and my family wasn't there. I walked in, called; there was no answer.

I drove over to Aunt Flo's to look for them and got caught in Sunday-morning rush hour. It was Confirmation Sunday at Lake Wobegon Lutheran Church. Thirteen young people had their faith confirmed and were admitted to the circle of believers, thirteen dressed-up boys and girls at the altar rail in front of a crowd of every available relative. Pastor Ingqvist asked them all the deepest questions about the faith (questions that have troubled theologians for years), which these young people answered readily from memory and then partook of their first communion. Later they lounged around on the front steps and asked each other, "Were you scared?" and said, "No, I really wasn't, not as much as I thought I'd be," and went home to eat chuck roast, and some of them had their first real cup of coffee. They found it to be a bitter oily drink that makes you dizzy and sick to your stomach, but they were Lutherans now and that's what Lutherans drink.

The Tolleruds, for example, drank gallons of coffee on Sunday. Church had been two hours long, the regular service plus confirmation, and Lutherans don't have the opportunity to stand up and kneel down and get exercise that you find elsewhere, so everyone was stiff and dopey, and the Tolleruds, when they sit around and visit, are all so quiet and agreeable they get drowsy, so they drink plenty of coffee. Years ago, when Uncle Gunnar was alive, they didn't need so much. He had wild white hair and eyebrows the size of mice, he spilled food down himself and didn't care, he had whiskey on his breath, and if anyone mentioned the Lutheran church he said, "Haw!" He was an old bachelor who got rich from founding a chain of private clubs in the Dakotas and Iowa called the Quality Prestige Clubs. They were only empty rooms over a drugstore with some old leather couches and a set of *Collier's Encyclopedia,* and he gave away memberships to men who'd never been invited to join a club before, tall sad men with thin dry hair, of whom there are a lot, and made his money selling them lots of shirts and ties and cufflinks with the QP insignia. Uncle Gunnar got rich and sold the Clubs to an Iowa meatpacker and went to Australia to get into some line of work down there he didn't consider worth mentioning, and the last anyone saw him was in 1962. Presumably he died, unless perhaps he just got tired of us knowing him.

The Tolleruds gathered for pot roast because Daryl and Marilyn's daughter Lois was confirmed. She sat at the head of the table, next to her dad, promoted from the children's table out in the kitchen. She is a tall lanky girl who has grown four inches this year, and it has tired her out. She is quieter than she used to be, a tall shy girl with long brown hair she has learned to tie in an elegant bun, and creamy skin that she keeps beautiful by frequent blushing, which is good for the circulation and makes her lovelier whenever she is admired.

A boy who has sat silently across from her in geometry since September has written her a twenty-seven-page letter in small print telling her how he feels about her (since September he's looked as if he was just about to talk, and now it all comes out at once: he thinks God has written their names together in the Book of Love). But she wasn't thinking about him Sunday—she was blushing to see her Confirmation cake with the Scripture verse inscribed in blue frosting: "Be not conformed to this world: but be ye transformed by the renewing of your mind, that ye may prove what is that good, and acceptable, and perfect, will of God." It was a large cake, and Marilyn used the extra-fine nozzle on the frosting gun—there it sat, lit with birthday candles, and Lois didn't know how to tell them that she wasn't sure that she believed in God. She was pretty sure that she might've lost her faith.

She thought she might've lost it on Friday night or sometime Saturday morning, she wasn't sure. She didn't mention it at that time because she thought she might get it back.

On Friday night, less than forty-eight hours before confirmation, she was sitting on the couch watching television with Dave, the boy who wrote the letter, while her mom and dad were gone to have supper with her prayer parents. When you're confirmed you're assigned prayer parents, a couple who promise to pray for you for three months prior, and Lois's turned out to be the Val Tollefsons, people she had never liked. To think that every night over supper Val Tollefson had bowed his big thick head and said, "And, Lord, we ask Thee to strengthen Lois in her faith"—the same man who said once, "You won't amount to a hill of beans, you don't have the sense that God gave geese." She could feel her faith slip a little. She felt guilty, because Dave wasn't supposed to be there, and she was supposed to be ironing her confirmation dress, but he had walked two miles from his house, so what could she do? She felt sorry for Dave, he always has a bad haircut and a swarm of pimples on his forehead, but she likes him, he's quiet and nice. They talked to each other at Luther League get-togethers about what it would be like to be someone else, someone famous, for example, like Willie Nelson—you could use your fame to do good—and they went for one walk halfway around the lake, holding hands, and then she got the long letter saying how much she meant to him, twenty-seven pages, which was much more than she wanted to mean to him; it scared her.

She didn't know that Dave was a born writer, that twenty-seven pages is nothing to him, he did thirty-one on the death of his dog, Buff—she told him it would be better if they didn't see each other anymore. Friday night he walked over, full of more to say. She had four little brothers and a sister to take care of, so he sat on the old red sofa with a bottle of orange pop and watched as she fed the baby, and she turned on the TV and lost her faith. Men in khaki suits were beating people senseless, shooting them with machine guns, throwing the bodies out of helicopters. Their reception was so poor, the picture so fuzzy, it was more like radio, which made the horrors worse, and she thought, "This could happen here." It gave her a cold chill to imagine violent strange men busting in, as they had done to

Anne Frank. She held the baby, Karen, imagining all of them were hiding from Nazis, and heard twigs crunch outside and knew that this boy could not protect her. She prayed and heard something like an echo, as if the prayer was only in her head. The whole world in the control of dark powers, working senseless evil on our lives, and prayer went no place, prayer just went up the chimney like smoke.

When Marilyn cut the confirmation cake and served it with butter-brickle ice cream, Lois thought, "I should say something." Like "I don't believe in God, I don't think." Nobody would need coffee then.

After dinner she put on her jeans and a white jacket and walked out across the cornfield toward the road and the ravine to think about her faith on this cloudy day, and, walking west over a little rise, she saw, just beyond the ravine, a white car she'd never seen before, and a strange man in a trenchcoat standing beside it. She walked toward him, thinking of the parable of the Good Samaritan, thinking that perhaps God was calling her to go witness to him and thereby recover her faith. He stood and pitched stones up over the trees, and as she got closer, he turned and smiled, put out his hand, and came toward her. She saw her mistake. Something glittered in his mouth. She stopped. He was a killer come looking for someone, it didn't matter to him who it was, anyone who came down the road would do. He walked toward her; she turned and fell down and said, "Oh please no, please God no."

I hadn't seen her for five years. I said, "Lois, Lois—it's me." I helped her up. How are you? It's good to see you again. We shuffled along the rim of the ravine, looking for the thin path down, and she told me about her confirmation, which I have an interest in because I am her godfather. I wasn't invited to church, I reckon, because fourteen years ago I wasn't anyone's first choice for godfather. I was nominated by Marilyn because Daryl suggested his brother Gunnar and she thought that was ridiculous, and to show Daryl what a poor choice he would be she suggested me, and Daryl said, "Sure, fine, if that's what you want," and they were stuck with me.

The baby was named for her mother's Sunday-school teacher, who was my aunt Lois, my youngest aunt, so young she was like an older sister. She was single when I was a boy and so had plenty of time for her favorite nephew. She told me I was. She said, Don't tell the others but you are the one I love more than anyone else, or words to that effect. We were riding the bus to Minneapolis, she and I, to visit Great-aunt Posie. Lois seemed young to me because she loved to pretend. We imagined the bus was our private bus and we could go anywhere we wanted. We were *somebody*.

My favorite game was Strangers, pretending we didn't know each other. I'd get up and walk to the back of the bus and turn around and come back to the seat and say, "Do you mind if I sit here?" And she said, "No, I don't mind," and I'd sit. And she'd say: "A very pleasant day, isn't it?"

We didn't speak this way in our family, but she and I were strangers, and so we could talk as we pleased.

"Are you going all the way to Minneapolis, then?"

"As a matter of fact, ma'am, I'm going to New York City. I'm in a very successful hit play on Broadway, and I came back out here to Minnesota because my sweet old aunt died, and I'm going back to Broadway now on the evening plane. Then next week I go to Paris, France, where I currently reside on the Champs-Elysées. My name is Tom Flambeau, perhaps you've read about me."

"No, I never heard of you in my life, but I'm very sorry to hear about your aunt. She must have been a wonderful person."

"Oh, she was pretty old. She was all right, I guess."

"Are you very close to your family, then?"

"No, not really. I'm adopted, you see. My real parents were Broadway actors—they sent me out to the farm thinking I'd get more to eat, but I don't think that people out here understand people like me."

She looked away from me. She looked out the window a long time. I'd hurt her feelings. Minutes passed. But I didn't know her. Then I said, "Talk to me. Please."

She said, "Sir, if you bother me anymore I'll have the driver throw you off this bus."

"Say that you know me. Please."

And when I couldn't bear it one more second, she touched me and I was myself again.

And the next time we rode the bus, I said, "Let's pretend we don't know each other."

She said, "No, you get too scared."

"I won't this time." I got up and came back and said, "It's a very pleasant day, isn't it? Are you going to Minneapolis?"

Eventually we do. We pretend to be someone else and need them to say they know us, but one day we become that person and they simply don't know us. From that there is no bus back that I know of.

Lois Tollerud asked me, "Why did you stop here?" I told her I had parked by the ravine, looking for a spot where our Boy Scout troop used to camp and where Einar Tingvold the scoutmaster got so mad at us once, he threw two dozen eggs one by one into the woods. Each egg made him madder and he threw it farther. When he ran out of eggs he reached for something else. It was his binoculars. He didn't want to throw them away but he was so furious he couldn't stop—he threw the binoculars and reached for them in the same motion. Heaved them and tried to grab the strap as it went by. We scouts looked for it for a whole afternoon, thirty years ago. Whenever I go by the ravine, I look for a reflection of glass, thinking that, if I found those binoculars by some wonderful luck and took them back to him, he might forgive me.

"That's not true, is it?" she said. "No, it's not."

I stopped there because, frankly, I'd had a lot of coffee, but I couldn't tell her that. We walked for almost a mile along that ravine, to the lake and back, and then I felt like I'd like to visit her family after all.

We walked in. I got a fairly warm hello, and was offered coffee. "In a minute," I said. "Excuse me, I'll be right back." I had a cup and a slice of cake that said "Con but for," a little triangle out of her verse.

Be not conformed to this world: but be ye transformed. Our lovely world has the power to make us brave. A person wants to be someone else and gets scared and needs to be known, but we ride so far on that bus, we become the stranger. Nevertheless these things stay the same: the sweet breath, the rain, the tendre croppes, and the smale fowles maken melodys—God watches each one and knows when it falls, and so much more does He watch us all.

Guides to Reflection

Exiles

1. Keillor purports to be telling stories of his hometown, but Lake Wobegon is an imaginary place. The stories, too, are made up; they are not true accounts of happenings in an actual town. One way that Keillor creates a sense of "truth" for the stories, though, is by pretending to visit this imaginary town and making himself a character in his stories. For instance, when Keillor describes "Larry the Sad Boy," who was saved twelve times at the Lutheran church, he says, "Even we fundamentalists got tired of him" (p. 120). How does this closeness of Keillor to the story affect your reaction to it? Think about this particularly in relation to the religious aspects of Keillor's story. How, for example, does it affect your response to his depiction of Larry to have Keillor identify himself as having been a member of a fundamentalist church?

2. Keillor "reports" that Father Emil's congregation was unusually quiet during his "hard homily," but then, at the end, Father Emil "said that this

was why Our Lord had come, to rescue us from dullness of spirit, and so the shepherds had found and so shall we, and then it was Christmas again" (p. 120). How is this "dullness of spirit" apparent in the story's characters? In what ways does Christmas affect that dullness? Are the characters' experiences like those of the shepherds at Bethlehem? Like your own experience? In what ways?

Aprille

1. Keillor includes in "Aprille" a number of people who are important to Lois and her crisis of faith: Dave, Val Tollefson, Uncle Gunnar, Keillor's Aunt Lois, and Keillor himself, who is Lois's godfather. How does each of these characters affect our understanding of Lois's faith, or lack of it? How do the stories about these other characters help us to see the full dimensions of Lois's crisis? What roles have these people played in Lois's family? What kind of religious faith do they each have? How does each one's faith, or lack of it, concern Lois?

2. Keillor begins "Aprille" by quoting the beginning of Geoffrey Chaucer's *Canterbury Tales,* a poem about thirty people on a pilgrimage in fourteenth century England. Journeys, long and short, recur in the story. Keillor has traveled to Lake Wobegon from the city where he lives, Uncle Gunnar has gone to Australia, Keillor describes bus trips he took as a boy with his Aunt Lois, and Lois, the confirmand, leaves her confirmation dinner to walk alone in the woods. These journeys all recall, in some way, Keillor's opening quotation. Think about the ways they relate to Keillor's theme of transformation in the story. Consider also how they might be seen as pilgrimages, which are journeys with spiritual dimensions.

3. Do you think Lois's crisis of faith at her confirmation is positive or negative? Typical or atypical? What would you have said to her in the woods were you, rather than the storyteller, her godparent?

Richard Rodriguez

Richard Rodriguez's essay "Credo" lies at the center of his autobiography, *Hunger of Memory: The Education of Richard Rodriguez*. Published in 1982, *Hunger of Memory* established Rodriguez as an important young writer. The book was widely reviewed in popular, scholarly, and religious journals, most notably on the front page of the *New York Times Book Review*—an impressive achievement for a writer, especially for a first book. A decade later, *Hunger of Memory* was in its sixth printing, and Rodriguez had written many essays and another book, *Days of Obligation*. He had become a contributing editor at *Harper's* and a commentator on public television's "MacNeil/Lehrer NewsHour."

In *Hunger of Memory*, Rodriguez showed himself to be, as one reviewer said, "a writer of unusual grace and clarity"[1]; he was also a writer willing to take risks. In the book, Rodriguez tells his compelling story of growing up in California, the child of Mexican immigrants. He evokes what he calls his "enchantedly happy"[2] childhood and reflects on the awkward loneliness that comes later as he and his siblings leave their private, intimate family world to enter the public world of American schools. But then, instead of dwelling solely on his personal experience, instead of giving his readers "more Grandma"[3] as his editor demanded, Rodriguez included in some sections of his book critiques of affirmative action and bilingual education programs, critiques that offended many of his reviewers. In fact, most reviewers for secular journals were so absorbed in discussing Rodriguez's political viewpoints, his immigrant experience, and his gifts as a prose writer that they ignored "Credo," at the heart of his book. Ironically, in reviewing *Hunger of Memory*, they adopted what Rodriguez calls in the book "the politesse of secular society concerning religion—say nothing about it."

In "Credo," this disjunction between Christianity and American culture, this silence, is one of Rodriguez's main subjects. He reflects on the place of his religious beliefs and experiences in his life as a child and as an adult. Throughout the essay, he returns again and again to the sense of discomfort he feels as a believer in a nonbelieving world. He is part of the modern, secular world in which most believers are "alone in their faith for most of the week." Then, on Sunday, they go to "half-empty churches," where each worshiper is "a stranger among strangers." Most of Rodriguez's colleagues, editors, and friends are surprised or even dismayed by his religious beliefs. One reviewer, for instance, commented: "Curiously enough, he remains a Catholic. He still goes to church on Sundays. He is that rare combination: an intellectual who is also a true believer."[4] A friend finds his Catholicism "a mere affectation, an attempt to play the Evelyn Waugh eccentric to a bland and vulgar secular age." Rodriguez assumes that, for the most part, his readers, too, do not share his religious commitment: "I am writing about my religious life, aware that most of my readers do not consider themselves religious."

Writing about his own religious life, Rodriguez addresses a problem that other writers and theologians also comment on: the difficulties many religious Americans face of being Christian in what is more and more often called a "post-Christian" culture. The theologians Stanley Hauerwas and William Willimon, for instance, conclude in their book *Resident Aliens* that "[i]n our day, unbelief is the socially acceptable way of living in the West"[5]; they remark on "how odd it is to be Christian"[6] in our culture. The novelist John Irving told an interviewer: "It is unfashionable for a literary figure to be a believer"; and "there is this intellectual assumption that to believe in the Christian thing is to be (intellectually) sub-par. . . . [to be] intellectually flawed."[7] The essayist Annie Dillard found it necessary to assert to an interviewer for *The New York Times Magazine:* "Just because I'm religious doesn't mean I'm insane."[8]

For a largely unsympathetic or uncomprehending audience, then, Rodriguez faces the challenge of articulating his religious beliefs and experiences in cogent ways. In his childhood those beliefs centered on his participation in church rituals, when sacred actions and words gave shape, definition, and meaning to his days: "the air was different, somehow still and more silent on Sundays and high feast days"; and he felt "lightened, transparent as sky" after confession. As an altar boy, Rodriguez felt the power and scope of worship, finding in it not the evasion of life that his secular friends assume is there, but rather a profound facing of it: "For my part, I will always be grateful to the Church that took me so seriously and exposed me so early, through the liturgy, to the experience of life."

When Rodriguez became an adult, the Roman Catholic liturgy had changed, and so too had he. Now in church, he finds a "ritual that seeks to feed my mind and would starve my somewhat metaphorical soul." Rodriguez recognizes in the changes the church's effort to speak to people in familiar ways. The new liturgies are the church's attempt to bridge the chasm between religious belief and contemporary culture. They are the result of the church attempting to address the questions of how to serve people who live in a secular world, how to worship God when God seems absent from so much of our lives. The temptation to decry the changes, to resist the new liturgies, is great for Rodriguez, as is, perhaps, the temptation for believers to shut themselves off from an unsympathetic, uncomprehending world, or to hide their beliefs when they venture into it.

In writing "Credo," Rodriguez brings into the public realm what is often relegated to the private. At the close of the essay, he expresses a deep longing and need for God: "If I should lose my faith in God, I would have no place to go to where I could feel myself a man. . . . If God is dead I will cry into the void." And, despite the secular world's lack of sympathy, he expresses a determination to find a "resolution to [his] spiritual dilemma" in it, among his friends, associates, and readers, among those who find his religious thought and commitment awkward, embarrassing, odd.

Paula J. Carlson

Notes

1. *New Yorker* 5 April 1982: 199.
2. *Hunger of Memory: The Education of Richard Rodriguez* (Boston: David Godine, 1982), 3.
3. *Hunger of Memory*, 7.
4. Carlos R. Hortas, review of *Hunger of Memory* in *Harvard Educational Review* 53 (1983): 355.
5. Stanley Hauerwas and William H. Willimon, *Resident Aliens: Life in the Christian Colony* (Nashville: Abingdon, 1989), 50.
6. *Resident Aliens*, 155.
7. "A Conversation with John Irving," *Image: A Journal of the Arts*, Summer 1992: 48.
8. Mary Cantwell, "A Pilgrim's Progress," *The New York Times Magazine*, 26 April 1992: 40.

Credo

The steps of the church defined the eternal square where children played and adults talked after dinner. He remembers the way the church building was at the center of town life. She remembers the way one could hear the bell throughout the day, telling time. And the way the town completely closed down for certain feastdays. He remembers that the church spire was the first thing he'd see walking back into town. Both my parents have tried to describe something of what it was like for them to have grown up Catholic in small Mexican towns. They remember towns where everyone was a Catholic.

With their move to America, my mother and father left behind that Mexican Church to find themselves (she praying in whispered Spanish) in an Irish-American parish. In a way, they found themselves at ease in such a church. My parents had much in common with the Irish-born priests and nuns. Like my parents, the priests remembered what it was like to have been Catholic in villages and cities where everyone else was a Catholic. In their American classrooms, the nuns worked very hard to approximate that other place, that earlier kind of religious experience. For a time they succeeded. For a time I too enjoyed a Catholicism something like that enjoyed by my parents.

I grew up a Catholic at home and at school, in private and in public. My mother and father were deeply pious *católicos*; all my relatives were Catholics. At home, there were holy pictures on a wall of nearly every room, and a crucifix hung over my bed. My first twelve years as a student were spent in Catholic schools where I could look up to the front of the room and see a crucifix hanging over the clock.

When I was a boy, anyone not a Catholic was defined by that fact and the term *non-Catholic*. The expression suggests the parochialism of the Catholicism in which I was raised. In those years I could have told you the names of persons in public life who were Catholics. I knew that Ed Sullivan was a Catholic. And Mrs. Bob Hope. And Senator John F. Kennedy. As the neighborhood newspaper boy, I knew all the names on my route. As a Catholic, I noted which open doors, which front room windows disclosed a crucifix. At quarter to eight Sunday mornings, I saw the O'Briens and the Van Hoyts walking down the empty sidewalk past our house and I knew. Catholics were mysteriously lucky, 'chosen' by God to be nurtured a special way. Non-Catholics had souls too, of course, and somehow could get to heaven. But on Sundays they got all dressed up only to go to a church where there was no incense, no sacred body and blood, and no confessional box. Or else they slept late and didn't go to church at all. For non-Catholics, it seemed, there was all white and no yolk.

In twelve years of Catholic schooling, I learned, in fact, very little about the beliefs of non-Catholics, though the little I learned was conveyed by my teachers without hostility and with fair accuracy. All that I knew about Protestants was that they differed from Catholics. But what precisely distinguished a Baptist from a Methodist from an Episcopalian I could not have said. I surmised the clearest notion of Protestant theology from discussions of the Reformation. At that, Protestantism emerged only as deviance from Catholic practice and thought. Judaism was different. Before the Christian era Judaism was *my* religion, the nuns said. ('We are all Jews because of Christ.') But what happened to Judaism after Christ's death to the time the modern state of Israel was founded, I could not have said. Nor did I know a thing about Hinduism or Buddhism or Islam. I knew nothing about modern secular ideologies. In civics class a great deal was said about oppressive Soviet policies; but at no time did I hear classical Marxism explained. In church, at the close of mass, the congregation prayed for 'the conversion of Russia.'

It is not enough to say that I grew up a ghetto Catholic. As a Catholic schoolboy, I was educated a middle-class American. Even while grammar school nuns reminded me of my spiritual separateness from non-Catholics, they provided excellent *public* schooling. A school day began with prayer— the Morning Offering. Then there was the Pledge of Allegiance to the American flag. Religion class followed immediately. But afterward, for the rest of the day, I was taught well those skills of numbers and words crucial to my Americanization. Soon I became as Americanized as my classmates— most of whom were two or three generations removed from their immigrant ancestors, and all of whom were children of middle-class parents.

When we were eleven years old, the nuns would warn us about the dangers of mixed marriage (between a Catholic and a non-Catholic). And we heard a priest say that it was a mortal sin to read newspaper accounts of a Billy Graham sermon. But the ghetto Catholic Church, so defensive, so fearful of contact with non-Catholics, was already outdated when I entered the classroom. My classmates and I were destined to live in a world very different from that which the nuns remembered in Ireland or my parents remembered in Mexico. We were destined to live on unhallowed ground, beyond the gated city of God.

I was in high school when Kennedy's picture went up on the wall. And I remember feeling that he was 'one of us.' His election to the presidency, however, did not surprise me as it did my father. Nor was I encouraged by it. I did not take it as evidence that Catholics could, after all, participate fully in American public life. (I assumed that to be true.) When I was a senior in high school, consequently, I did not hesitate to apply to secular colleges.

It was to be in college, at Stanford, that my religious faith would seem to me suddenly pared. I would remain a Catholic, but a Catholic defined by a non-Catholic world. This is how I think of myself now. I remember my early Catholic schooling and recall an experience of religion very different from anything I have known since. Never since have I felt so much at home in the Church, so easy at mass. My grammar school years especially were the years when the great Church doors opened to enclose me, filling my day as I was certain the Church filled all time. Living in a community of shared faith, I enjoyed much more than mere social reinforcement of religious belief. Experienced continuously in public and private, Catholicism shaped my whole day. It framed my experience of eating and sleeping and washing; it named the season and the hour.

The sky was full then and the coming of spring was a religious event. I would awaken to the sound of garage doors creaking open and know without thinking that it was Friday and that my father was on his way to six-thirty mass. I saw, without bothering to notice, statues at home and at school of the Virgin and of Christ. I would write at the top of my arithmetic or history homework the initials Jesus, Mary, and Joseph. (All my homework was thus dedicated.) I felt the air was different, somehow still and more silent on Sundays and high feastdays. I felt lightened, transparent as sky, after confessing my sins to a priest. Schooldays were routinely divided by prayers said with classmates. I would not have forgotten to say grace before eating. And I would not have turned off the light next to my bed or fallen asleep without praying to God.

1*

. . . .

2

Of all the institutions in their lives, only the Catholic Church has seemed aware of the fact that my mother and father are thinkers—persons aware

---

*Section 1 of "Credo" has been omitted with permission of the publisher.

of the experience of their lives. Other institutions—the nation's political parties, the industries of mass entertainment and communications, the companies that employed them—have all treated my parents with condescension. The Church too has treated them badly when it attempted formal instruction. The homily at Sunday mass, intended to give parishioners basic religious instruction, has often been poorly prepared and aimed at a childish listener. It has been the liturgical Church that has excited my parents. In ceremonies of public worship, they have been moved, assured that their lives—all aspects of their lives, from waking to eating, from birth until death, all moments—possess great significance. Only the liturgy has encouraged them to dwell on the meaning of their lives. To think.

What the Church gave to my mother and father, it gave to me. During those years when the nuns warned me about the dangers of intellectual pride and referred to Christ as Baby Jesus, they were enabling me to participate fully in the liturgical life of the Church. The nuns were not interested in constructing a temple of religious abstractions. God was more than an idea; He was person—white-bearded, with big arms. (Pictures could not show what He really was like, the nuns said, but one could be sure that He was Our Father.) He loved us and we were to respond, like children, in love. Our response would be prayer.

In my first-grade classroom I learned to make the sign of the cross with English words. In addition to prayers said at home (prayers before dinner and before sleeping), there were prayers in the classroom. A school day was divided by prayer. First, the Morning Offering. At 10:15, before recess, the Prayer to My Guardian Angel. At noontime, the Angelus, in celebration of the Word: 'The angel of the Lord declared unto Mary . . .' After lunch came the Creed. And before going home the Act of Contrition. In first grade I was taught to make the sign of the cross when I entered the church. And how to genuflect (the right knee bending and touching all the way to the floor). And the nuns told us of the most perfect prayer (Christ's offering of His body and blood to the Father), the 'sacrifice' of the mass.

Alongside red, yellow, blue, green, Dick and Jane, was disclosed to us the knowledge of our immortal souls. And that our souls (we were Catholics) needed the special nourishment of the Church—the mass and the sacraments.

In second grade, at the age of seven, we were considered by the Church to have reached the age of reason; we were supposed capable of distinguishing good from evil. We were able to sin; able to ask forgiveness for sin. In second grade, I was prepared for my first Confession, which took place on a Saturday morning in May. With all my classmates, I went to the unlit church where the nun led us through the forms of an 'examination of conscience.' Then, one by one—as we would be summoned to judgment after death—we entered the airless confessional. The next day—spotless souls—we walked as a class up the aisle of church, the girls in white dresses and veils like small brides, the boys in white pants and white shirts. We walked to the altar rail where the idea of God assumed a shape and a scent and a taste.

As an eight-year-old Catholic, I learned the names and functions of all seven sacraments. I knew why the priest put glistening oil on my grandmother's forehead the night she died. At the baptismal font I watched a baby cry out as the priest trickled a few drops of cold water on his tiny red forehead. At ten I knew the meaning of the many ritual gestures the priest makes during the mass. I knew (by heart) the drama of feastdays and seasons—and could read the significance of changing altar cloth colors as the year slowly rounded.

The Church rocked through time—a cradle, an ark—to rhythms of sorrow and joy, marking the passage of man.

The Catholic calendar in my bedroom was printed by W. F. Gormley and Sons, morticians. Every month there was a different Bible picture in beautiful colors. Every day was something. The calendar noted ferial and ember days, fish days and the feastdays of saints. (My birthday honored St. Ignatius Loyola.) There was another, a 'regular,' calendar in the kitchen (Capitol Savings and Loan). It noted full moons and crescents and the official change of the seasons. My mother used the regular calendar to write down our doctors' appointments (shots; teeth).

It was the religious calendar that governed my school year. In early September there was a nine o'clock mass on the Friday of the first week of school to pray for academic success. (Students were grouped according to class; behind my class would be my new teacher's face, a face I still wasn't used to.) In June, there was a Mass of graduation for the eighth-graders. Between those events, school often stopped or flowered as routine bowed to the sacred. In the middle of a geography or an arithmetic lesson, the nuns would lead us out of our classrooms and we would walk—four hundred students in double lines—down a block to church, stopping traffic (We were Catholics!) to attend a First Friday mass or a rosary to Mary. In Lent there were Friday Stations of the Cross. (Fourteen meditations on the passion of Christ—He stumbled, He fell—fourteen times the priest intoning, 'We adore Thee, O Christ. . . .') Benediction, the adoration of the Host, followed. The lovely hymn, the *Tantum Ergo* sounded as smoke of incense rose like vine. Upon the high altar stood a golden monstrance in the shape of a sunburst, at the center of which—exposed through a tiny window—was the round wafer of bread. We returned to the classroom, came back to the same paragraph in a still-opened book. Routine resumed. Sacred dramas of Church thus fitted into a day, never became the routine; rather they redeemed the routine.

On Halloween night, all over Sacramento, children dressed up as ghosts or Frankensteins or dime-store skeletons with phosphorescent bones. But only Catholic school kids went to mass the next morning to honor the white-robed saints on the Feast of All Hallows. It was one of the 'holy days of obligation'—a day on which I was obliged to go to morning mass, but for the rest of the day I was free—no school. I could ride my bicycle around Sacramento; watch public school kids walking to school. And people downtown were passing just another day. (They seemed not to know.)

In the secular calendar there was no day like Ash Wednesday. All day I would see on the heedless foreheads of classmates the Hindu-like smudge of dark ash, the reminder of death. (. . . Unto dust thou shalt return.) One year a girl at school was killed in a car crash shortly after Ash Wednesday. I took the lesson.

On those few occasions when secular Sacramento took up the sacred calendar they got it all wrong. Christmas downtown began in early November. Merchants would string tiny white lights up over K Street, where they shone through the night as pretty as heaven. But their Christmas ended in late afternoon on Christmas Eve—I saw department store clerks working against time to replace a holiday window display with deathly white piles of towels and sheets. In church, in early November there was Advent, the time for penance. On a table in front of the altar was a wreath with four candles stuck in, one of which was lit each week to mark the coming—the slow, slow coming—of Christ. In church, Christmas began at midnight mass, Christmas Eve. And the holy season continued until the Feast of Epiphany, the sixth of January, when carols were sung for the very last time and fir trees on the altar no longer cast their dark scent of damp earth.

The secular calendar whirled like a carnival wheel and offered carnival prizes—a fat Santa instead of the infant God; colored eggs and chocolate bunnies instead of the death and resurrection of Christ. During Holy Week all pictures and statues in church were shrouded by purple silk drapes. On Holy Thursday to commemorate the Last Supper of Christ there was a 'white' mass at sunset (when stained-glass windows burned briefly before the light failed). After that mass, the sacrament was removed to a side altar and the red sanctuary lamp was extinguished, so that the next day, Good Friday, when women in scarves and men in work clothes came to church for 'the three hours' they found an altar stripped bare and the tabernacle gaping.

In our house on Good Friday we behaved as if a member of our family had died. There was no radio or television. But I noticed that the Standard gas station right across from church stayed open for business as usual and I saw people at the Laundromat watching their clothes tumble behind a round window—as if nothing in the world had happened. In Sacramento, the blue Easter morning seemed always to rhyme with the gospel account of the three Marys wending their way through a garden to discover an empty tomb. At church, at the altar, there were vestments of gold and the climbing voices of a Mozart mass, tossing rings sempiternal.

The wheels turned. Two wheels of time. The secular calendar made plain note of the hot first day of summer. Fall. Then winter. Ordinary time: Labor Day. The first day of school. Arithmetic class. An hour for spelling (a test every Friday). Recess. Church time: Benediction with classmates. Candles on St. Blaise's day. Ash. Palms in April. The red-eyed white dove descending, descending on Pentecost Sunday. Mary crowned with dying sweet flowers on the first day of May. The wheels turned. Second grade. Third grade. Fifth grade. Christmas. Epiphany. The secular calendar announced the vernal equinox. The low valley fog of late winter would slowly yield to the coming of Easter.

I went to the nine o'clock mass every Sunday with my family. At that time in my life, when I was so struck by diminished family closeness and the necessity of public life, church was a place unlike any other. It mediated between my public and private lives. I would kneel beside my brother and sisters. On one side of us would be my mother. (I could hear her whispered Spanish Hail Mary.) On the other side, my father. In the pew directly in front of us were the Van Hoyts. And in front of them were the druggist and his family. Over to the side was a lady who wore fancy dresses, a widow who prayed a crystal rosary. She was alone, as was the old man in front who cupped his face in his hands while he prayed. It was this same gesture of privacy the nuns would teach me to use, especially after Communion when I thanked God for coming into my soul.

The mass mystified me for being a public and a private event. We prayed here, each of us, much as we prayed on our pillows—most privately—all alone before God. And yet the great public prayer of the mass would go on. No one ever forgot where they were. People stood up together or they knelt at the right time in response to the progression of the liturgy. Every Sunday in summer someone fainted from heat, had to be carried out, but the mass went on.

I remember being puzzled very early by how different things were for the Protestants. Evangelical Christians would ring the doorbell to ask bluntly whether or not I was 'saved.' They proceeded to tell me about their own conversions to Christ. From classmates I would hear about Holy Rollers who jumped up and down and even fell to the floor at their services. It was funny. Hard to believe. My religion—the true religion—was so different. On Sunday afternoons, for a guilty few minutes, I'd watch an Oral Roberts prayer meeting on television. Members of the congregation made public confessions of sin, while people off camera shouted, 'Hallelujah, sister! Hallelujah, brother, preach it!'

Sister and *Brother* were terms I used in speaking to my teachers for twelve years. *Father* was the name for the priest at church. I never confused my teachers or the priests with actual family members; in fact they were most awesome for being without families. Yet I came to use these terms with ease. They implied that a deep bond existed between my teachers and me as fellow Catholics. At the same time, however, *Sister* and *Father* were highly formal terms of address—they were titles, marks of formality like a salute or a curtsey. (One would never have spoken to a nun without first calling her Sister.) It was possible consequently to use these terms and to feel at once a close bond, and the distance of formality. In a way, that is how I felt with all fellow Catholics in my world. We were close— somehow related—while also distanced by careful reserve.

Not once in all the years of my Catholic schooling did I hear a classmate or teacher make a public confession. ('Public' confessions were whispered through darkness to the shadow of a priest sworn to secrecy.) Never once did I hear a classmate or teacher make an exclamation of religious joy. Religious feelings and faith were channeled through ritual. Thus it was that my classmates and I prayed easily throughout the school day. We recited sublime prayers and childish ones ('Angel of God, my guardian dear . . .') And nobody snickered. Because the prayers were always the same and because they were said by the group, we had a way of praying together without being self-conscious.

Children of ceremony: My classmates and I would rehearse our roles before major liturgical celebrations. Several days before a feastday we would learn the movements for a procession. In the half-darkened church one nun stood aside with a wooden clapper which she knocked to tell us when to rise, when to kneel, when to leave the pew, when to genuflect ('All together!'). We'd rehearse marching (the tallest last) up the aisle in straight, careful lines. Worship was managed as ceremony.

My sense of belonging in this ceremonial Church was dearest when I turned twelve and became an altar boy. Dressed in a cassock like a priest's

I assisted at the performance of mass on the altar. It was my responsibility to carry the heavy red missal back and forth from one side of the altar to the other; to pour water and sweet-scented wine into the priest's chalice; to alert the congregation with a handbell at the *Sanctus* and at the elevation of the Host. But by far the greatest responsibility was to respond to the priest in memorized Latin prayers. I served as the voice of the congregation, sounding, all told, perhaps a hundred responsorial lines.

Latin, the nuns taught us, was a universal language. One could go into a Catholic church anywhere in the world and hear the very same mass. But Latin was also a dead language, a tongue foreign to most Catholics. As an altar boy, I memorized Latin in blank envelopes of sound: *Ad day um qui lay tee fee cat u ven tu tem may um.* Many of the 'ordinary' prayers of the mass were generally recognizable to me. (Any Catholic who used a bilingual missal could, after a while, recognize the meaning of whole prayers like the *Credo.*) I had the advantage of being able to hear in the shrouded gallery of Latin sounds echoes of Spanish words familiar to me. Listening to a priest I could often grasp the general sense of what he was saying—but I didn't always try to. In part, Latin permitted escape from the prosaic world. Latin's great theatrical charm, its sacred power, was that it could translate human aspiration to a holy tongue. The Latin mass, moreover, encouraged private reflection. The sounds of Latin would sometimes blur my attention to induce an aimless drift inward. But then I would be called back by the priest's voice (*'Oremus . . .'*) to public prayer, the reminder that an individual has the aid of the Church in his life. I was relieved of the burden of being alone before God through my membership in the Church.

Parish priests recognized and encouraged my fascination with the liturgy. During the last three years of grammar school, I was regularly asked to 'serve' as an altar boy. In my busiest year, eighth grade, I served at over two hundred masses. I must have served at about thirty baptisms and about the same number of weddings and funerals. During the school year I was excused from class for an hour or two to serve at a funeral mass. In summertime I would abandon adolescence to put the black cassock of mourning over a light summer shirt. A spectator at so many funerals, I grew acquainted with the rhythms of grief. I knew at which moments, at which prayers in church and at gravesides, survivors were most likely to weep. I studied faces. I learned to trust the grief of persons who showed no emotion. With the finesse of a mortician, I would lead mourners to the grave. I helped carry coffins (their mysterious weight—neither heavy nor light) to burial sites when there were not mourners enough. And then I would return. To class or to summer. Resume my life as a boy of thirteen.

There are people who tell me today that they are not religious because they consider religion to be an evasion of life. I hear them, their assurance, and do not bother to challenge the arrogance of a secular world which hasn't courage enough to accept the fact of old age. And death. I know people who speak of death with timorous euphemisms of 'passing away.' I have friends who wouldn't think of allowing their children to attend a funeral for fear of inflicting traumatic scars. For my part, I will always be grateful to the Church that took me so seriously and exposed me so early, through the liturgy, to the experience of life. I will always be grateful to the parish priest who forced a mortician to remove an elaborate arrangement of flowers from a coffin: 'Don't hide it!'

I celebrate now a childhood lived through the forms of the liturgical Church. As the Church filled my life, I grew to the assurance that my life, my every action and thought, was important for good or for bad. Bread and wine, water, oil, salt, and ash—through ceremonies of guilt and redemption, sorrow and rebirth, through the passing liturgical year, my boyhood assumed all significance. I marvel most at having so easily prayed with others—not simply alone. I recall standing at the altar at Easter, amid candles and gold vestments, hearing the Mozart high mass. These were impossible riches. I remember wanting to cry out with joy, to shout. I wanted to shout. But I didn't, of course. I worshipped in a ceremonial church, one in a group. I remained silent and remembered to genuflect exactly on cue. After the mass, I pulled off the surplice and cassock and rushed to meet my parents, waiting for me in front of the church. 'It was very nice today,' my mother said. Something like that. 'It makes you feel good, the beautiful music and everything.' That was all that she said. It was enough.

3

Now. I go to mass every Sunday. Old habits persist. But it is an English mass I attend, a ritual of words. A ritual that seeks to feed my mind and would starve my somewhat metaphorical soul. The mass is less ornamental; it has been 'modernized,' tampered with, demythologized, deflated. The priest performs fewer gestures. His central role as priest—intermediary between congregation and God—is diminished. Symbols have changed. A reciprocal relationship between people and clergy is dramatized as the congregation takes an active role in the recitation of the mass. The priest faces the people, his back to the tabernacle. And the effect of this rearrangement is to make the mass seem less a prayer directed to God, more a communal celebration of the Eucharist. There is something occasional about it all, and no occasion for pomp or solemnity. No longer is the congregation moved to a contemplation of the timeless. Rather it is the idiomatic one hears. One's focus is upon this place. This time. The moment. Now.

In the old Latin mass my mother could recite her rosary while still being at one with prayer at the altar. The new English mass is unilinear, lacking density; there is little opportunity for private prayer. The English words enforce attention. Emphasis is on the communal prayer, communal identity. There is a moment just before the Communion when members of the congregation shake hands to dramatize a union. We nod and bow, shake hands like figures on a music box.

I go along with the Kiss of Peace, but paradoxically I feel isolated sitting in half-empty churches among people I am suddenly aware of not knowing. The kiss signifies to me a betrayal of the older ceremonial liturgy. I miss that high ceremony. I am saddened by inappropriate music about which it is damning enough to say that it is not good enough, and not even the best of its authentic kind—folk, pop, quasi-religious Broadway show tunes. I miss the old trappings—trappings that disclosed a different reality. I have left church early, walked out, after hearing the congregation spontaneously applaud its own singing. And I have wondered how the Church I loved could have changed so quickly and completely.

I continue to claim my Catholicism. Invariably I arrive late at somebody's brunch or tennis party—the festivities of a secular Sunday. Friends find it peculiar that I still go to mass; most have heard me complain about liturgical changes. Amid the orange juice and croissants I burlesque the folk-mass liturgy ('Kumbaya'), the peppy tambourine. Those listening find my sarcasm amusing. And someone says that my Catholicism is a mere affectation, an attempt to play the Evelyn Waugh eccentric to a bland and vulgar secular age.

I am not surprised. I do not know myself, not with any certainty, how much I really am saying when I profess Catholicism. In a cultural sense, I remain a Catholic. My upbringing has shaped in me certain attitudes which have not worn thin over the years. I am, for example, a materialist largely because I was brought up to believe in the central mystery of the Church—the redemptive Incarnation. (I carried the heavy gold crucifix in church ceremonies far too often to share the distrust of the material still prevalent in modern Puritan America.) I am a man who trusts a society that is carefully ordered by figures of authority. (I respond to policemen in the same tone of voice I used years ago, addressing parish priests and nuns.) I realize that I am a Catholic, moreover, when I listen skeptically to a political thinker describe with enthusiasm a scheme for lasting political change. (My historical pessimism was determined by grammar school lessons about sin, especially Original Sin.)

More important than any of this, I continue to believe the central tenets of the Church. I stand at the Creed of the mass. Though it is exactly then, at that very moment in the liturgy, when I must realize how different the Church has become in recent years. I stand as a stranger among strangers. For the truth is: It is not only the Church that has changed; I've changed as well.

My Catholicism changed when I was in high school. The liturgy was just then beginning to be altered. It was not simply that I found a different Church when I went to church; I went to church less often. (My high school was not connected to a neighborhood church the way my grammar school had been. There were, consequently, few schooldays interrupted by worship.) Liturgy was something for Sunday.

My high school, staffed by the Christian Brothers, offered a more 'Protestant' education. My freshman literature teacher only smiled when I mentioned the grammar school incident concerning Flaubert. He and other high school teachers encouraged my intellectual independence. Religious instruction became rigorously intellectual. With excitement I'd study complex Pauline and Thomistic theology and I'd remember with something like scorn the simple instructions of *The Baltimore Catechism*. In high school I started saying that *I believed* in Catholicism. My faith was buttressed by a book by Jacques Maritain rather than by the experience of worship at a Lenten service with classmates or serving at some old lady's funeral. Those years were marked by the realization that my parents assumed a Catholicism very different from mine. My parents seemed to me piously simple—like the nuns I remembered—unwilling to entertain intellectual challenges. They would rely on their rosary every night, while in another room I read patristic theology.

In college I had few Catholic friends and fewer Catholic teachers. Most of my friends had been raised as Protestants or Jews; many referred to themselves as agnostics. During my college years I started reading Protestant theology. The Church was no longer my sole spiritual teacher. I blended Catholicism with borrowed insights from Sartre and Zen and Buber and Miltonic Protestantism. And Freud.

I was a senior at Stanford during the last year of the Vatican Council. I cheered for the liberal bishops and cardinals at that great convocation. (The villains, in my view, were the conservatives of the Roman Curia.) I welcomed the Church's attempts at reconciliation with other religions. I approved of the liberal encyclicals concerning 'the Church in the modern world.' But I was changing rather more quickly than the Council fathers were changing the Church. I was already a 'new Catholic.' I didn't wait for the American bishops to terminate the observance of meatless Fridays before I ate what looked best in the dormitory cafeteria on Friday nights. Nor did I request a dispensation from a priest when a non-Catholic friend asked me to be his best man. I simply agreed and stood beside him in a Methodist church.

I would go to friends for advice when I was troubled; I didn't go to priests anymore. I stopped going to Confession, not because my behavior conflicted with the teachings of the institutional Church but because I no longer thought to assess my behavior against those standards. A Catholic who lived most of his week without a sense of communal Catholicism, I relied upon conscience as never before. The priest who was the college chaplain would regularly say in his sermons that a Catholic must rely upon conscience as his ultimate guide. It seemed so to me. But I remember feeling uneasy when that priest was later excommunicated for having been secretly married.

Throughout college and graduate school, I thought of myself as an orthodox Catholic. I was a liberal Catholic. In all things save the liturgy I was a liberal. From the start I despised the liturgical reformation. In college chapels I would listen to folk singing and see plain altars draped with bright applique banners: JOY! GOD IS LOVE. One Sunday I would watch dancers in leotards perform some kind of ballet in front of the altar; one Sunday there would be a rock mass; one Sunday the priest encouraged us to spend several minutes before the Offertory introducing ourselves, while a small bad jazzy combo punched out a cocktail mix. I longed for the Latin mass. Incense. Music of Bach. Ceremonies of candles and acolytes.

Over the last several years, I have visited many Catholic churches in the several cities I have lived in. Palo Alto. New York. Berkeley. Los Angeles. London. San Francisco. I have wandered on Sundays from church to church. But in all the churches I have had to listen to the new English mass. The proclamation of faith, the Creed, I hear recited by the congregation around me. 'We believe in God. . . .' In the abandoned Latin service it was the priest alone who spoke the affirmation of faith. It was the priest who said, '*Credo* . . . ,' using the first person singular. The differences between the old service and the new can be summarized in this change. At the old mass, the priest's *Credo* (I believe) complexly reminded the congregation of the fact that each person stands before God as an individual, implying at the same time—because the priest could join all voices in his—the union of believers, the consolation of communal faith. The listener was assured of his membership in the Church; he was not alone before God. (The

Church would assist him.) By translating *credo* into the English first person plural, *we* believe, the Church no longer reminds the listener that he is alone. 'We believe,' the congregation is encouraged to say, celebrating community—but only that fact.

I would protest this simplification of the liturgy if I could. I would protest as well the diminished sense of the sacred in churches today. I would protest the use of folk music and the hand-holding. Finally, I cannot. I suspect that the reason I despise the new liturgy is because it is mine. It reflects and attempts to resolve the dilemma of Catholics just like me. The informal touches; the handshaking; the folk music; the insistence upon union—all these changes are aimed at serving Catholics who no longer live in a Catholic world. To such Catholics—increasingly alone in their faith—the Church says: You are part of a community of believers. You are not single in your faith. Not solitary. We are together, Catholics. *We* believe. We believe. We believe. This assurance is necessary because, in a sense, it no longer is true.

The Catholic Church of my past required no such obvious reminders of community as smiles and handshakes before the Communion. The old mass proceeded with sure, blind pomp precisely because Catholics had faith in their public identity as Catholics; the old liturgy was ceremonial because of the Church's assumption that worship is a public event. The lack of high ceremony in church today betrays a loss of faith in communal Catholicism. In obvious ways everyone in the congregation seems closer and more aware of each other. As a group, throughout mass, the congregation responds to the priest with various prayers; one listens to a steady flow of prayers said in English. But there is scant opportunity for private prayer. The Church cannot dare it.

A priest I once heard in a white middle-class parish defended the reformed liturgy by saying that it had become necessary to 'de-Europeanize' the Roman Catholic Church. He said that Catholicism must translate God's Word into the many languages and cultures of the world. I suppose he is right. I do not think, however, that the primary impetus for liturgical reformation came from Third World Catholics. I think rather that it came in response to a middle-class crisis of faith in North America and Western Europe. The new liturgy is suited especially to those who live in the secular city, alone in their faith for most of the week. It is not a liturgy suited to my parents or grandparents as much as to me.

When I go to church on Sunday I am forced to recognize a great deal about myself. I would rather go to a high ceremonial mass, reap for an hour or two its communal assurance. The sentimental solution would be ideal: to remain a liberal Catholic and to worship at a traditional mass.

But now that I no longer live as a Catholic in a Catholic world, I cannot expect the liturgy—which reflects and cultivates my faith—to remain what it was. I will continue to go to the English mass. I will go because it is my liturgy. I will, however, often recall with nostalgia the faith I have lost. And I will be uneasy knowing that the old faith was lost as much by *choice* as it was inevitably lost. My education may have made it inevitable that I would become a citizen of the secular city, but I have come to *embrace* the city's values: social mobility; pluralism; egalitarianism; self-reliance. By choice I do not confine myself to Catholic society. Most of my friends and nearly all of my intimates are non-Catholics. With them I normally will observe the politesse of secular society concerning religion—say nothing about it. By choice I do not pray before eating lunch in a downtown restaurant. (My public day is not divided by prayer.) By choice I do not consult the movie ratings of the Legion of Decency, and my reading is not curtailed by the Index. By choice I am ruled by conscience rather than the authority of priests I consider my equals. I do not listen to papal pronouncements with which I disagree.

Recently, bishops and popes who have encouraged liturgical reforms have seemed surprised at the insistence of so many Catholics to determine for themselves the morality of such matters as divorce, homosexuality, contraception, abortion, and extramarital sex. But the Church fathers who initiated rituals that reflect a shared priesthood of laity and clergy should not be surprised by the independence of modern Catholics. The authoritarian Church belonged to another time. It was an upper-class Church; it was a lower-class Church. It was a hierarchical Church. It was my grandparents' Church.

If I ask questions about religion that my grandparents didn't ask, it is not because I am intellectually advanced. I wonder about the existence of God because, unlike my grandparents, I live much of my day in a secular city where I do not measure the hours with the tolling bells of a church. As a boy, I believed in God by believing in His Church. Now that my faith in communal Catholicism is so changed, my faith in God is without certain foundation. It occurs to me to ask that profound question of modern agnosticism: Is God dead?

I would cry into the void. . . . If I should lose my faith in God, I would have no place to go to where I could feel myself a man. The Catholic Church of my youth mediated with special grace between the public and private realms of my life, such was the extent of its faith in itself. That Church is no longer mine. I cling to the new Catholic Church. Though it leaves me unsatisfied, I fear giving it up, falling through space. Even in today's Catholic Church, it is possible for me to feel myself in the eye of God, while I kneel in the presence of others.

If God is dead, where shall I go for such an experience? In this modern post-religious age, secular institutions flounder to imitate the gift that is uniquely found in the temple and mosque and church. Secular institutions lack the key; they have no basis for claiming access to the realm of the private. When they try to deny their limits, secular institutions only lie. They pretend that there is no difference between public and private life. The worst are totalitarian governments. They respect no notion of privacy. They intrude into a family's life. They ignore the individual's right to be private. They would bulldoze the barrier separating the public from the private. They create the modern nightmare of institutional life.

If God is dead I will cry into the void.

There was a time in my life when it would never have occurred to me to make a confession like this one. There was a time when I would never have thought to discuss my spiritual life—even with other Catholics I knew intimately. It is true that in high school I read Augustine's *Confessions,* but that extraordinary autobiography did not prompt my imitation. Just the reverse: There seemed to me something non-Catholic about the Confessions. I intuited that such revelations made Augustine a Protestant church father more than a Catholic father.

Years after, in college, I remember reading the diaries of seventeenth-century Puritans. To encounter 'simple' people—a tradesman, a housewife, a farmer—describing their spiritual lives in detail amazed me. The Protestant confession was boldly different from the Catholic sacrament of Confession. The Protestants were public about their spiritual lives in a way that I, as a Catholic schoolboy, could never have been. Protestants were so public because they were otherwise alone in their faith. I marveled at the paradox implied by their writings. Those early 'pure' English Protestants, strangers to ceremony, and for their own reasons alien from the institutional Church, were attempting to form through their writings, a new kind of Christian community—a community of those who share with each other *only* the experience of standing alone before God. It was then that I began to realize the difference separating the individualistic Protestant from the institutional Catholic. Now I realize that I have become like a Protestant Christian. I call myself a Christian.

My own Catholic Church in recent years has become more like a Protestant Church. Perhaps Protestants will teach Catholics how to remain believers when the sense one has for so much of one's day is of being alone in faith. If, in fact, my spiritual fathers are those seventeenth-century

Puritans, there is one important difference between their writings and mine. I am writing about my religious life, aware that most of my readers do not consider themselves religious. With them—with you—I am making this admission of faith. It is appropriate that I do so. The resolution of my spiritual dilemma, if there is to be one before death, will have to take place where it began, among persons who do not share my religious convictions. Persons like my good friends now, those who, smiling, wonder why I am more than an hour late for their Sunday brunch.

Guides to Reflection

1. Rodriguez titles this essay "Credo," a Latin word meaning "I believe." "Credo" begins the Apostles' and Nicene Creeds, which Rodriguez describes reciting during worship before and after the liturgical changes instituted in the Roman Catholic Church in the late 1960s. "Credo" has also come to mean in English a person's personal beliefs or personal creed. How does Rodriguez use these two meanings of the word in his essay? Why do you think he titles the piece "Credo"? How would you describe the "credo" he presents in the essay?

2. Rodriguez uses the metaphors of a cradle and an ark to describe the Church: "The Church rocked through time—a cradle, an ark—to rhythms of sorrow and joy, marking the passage of man" (p. 138). In contrast, he says, "the secular calendar whirled like a carnival wheel and offered carnival prizes" (p. 139). Consider the ways these different images—cradle, ark, carnival wheel—reveal and reinforce the differences between the sacred and secular worlds in Rodriguez's childhood. What associations with the movements and purposes of cradles, arks, and carnival wheels is Rodriguez relying on to communicate his meaning? Do these contrasting images make sense to you? Why or why not?

3. Rodriguez describes his experiences of the tension between Christianity and culture in large cities: "Palo Alto. New York. Berkeley. Los Angeles. London. San Francisco" (p. 146). The examples that Hauerwas and Willimon use in their book, though, are almost all from small cities or towns in the American South. They begin their book, for instance, by recounting the experience of a teenager in 1963 sneaking out of church in his hometown of Greenville, South Carolina, to go to the movie theater on the first Sunday it opened in the morning. Think about Rodriguez's critique of Christianity and culture in terms of what you know about churches in the place you

live. Has religion become "disestablished," or cut off from other aspects of the community's life? To what degree? Have Christians become "alien"?

4. The liturgical changes in the churches where Rodriguez worships leave him feeling unsatisfied. What are the bases for this discomfort? Why does he rue the changes? What does he see church officials as having neglected in making the changes? How do you respond to Rodriguez's critique of new liturgies?

5. How do you answer Jesus' question in Mark 8:29? How does your answer reflect your view of culture, church, and Christianity?

Discover God's Presence in
Listening for God

Never before has a resource touched upon the issues of life and faith in such a personal way. Excellent contemporary literature helps one realize the presence of God in many places and relationships. Each volume of *Listening for God* includes excerpts from the works of eight contemporary authors, supplemented by author profiles and reflection questions. Each volume has a companion video with interviews introducing the authors featured in the Reader. A Leader Guide, offering suggestions for organizing class time and responding to reflection questions, is packaged with each video and is also available separately. *Contributing editors: Paula J. Carlson and Peter S. Hawkins.*

Volume 1

Reader, Volume 1 • 0-8066-2715-8
Wonderful selections from Flannery O'Connor, Frederick Buechner, Patricia Hampl, Raymond Carver, Annie Dillard, Alice Walker, Garrison Keillor, and Richard Rodriguez.

Leader Guide, Volume 1 • 0-8066-2716-6
Videocassette, Volume 1 • 0-8066-2717-4

Volume 2

Reader, Volume 2 • 0-8066-2844-8
Discover new ideas and insights in selections from John Updike, Anne Tyler, Henry Louis Gates, Jr., Tobias Wolff, Carol Bly, Gail Godwin, Kathleen Norris, and Andre Dubus.

Leader Guide, Volume 2 • 0-8066-2845-6
Videocassette, Volume 2 • 0-8066-2846-4

Volume 3

Reader, Volume 3 • 0-8066-3962-8
Includes selections from John Cheever, Mary Gordon, Wendell Berry, Oscar Hijuelos, Reynolds Price, Louise Erdrich, Tess Gallagher, and Tillie Olsen.

Leader Guide, Volume 3 • 0-8066-3963-6
Videocassette, Volume 3 • 0-8066-4597-0

Volume 4

Reader, Volume 4 • 0-8066-4577-6
Features essays and stories from Michael Malone, James Baldwin, Sue Miller, Kent Haruf, Doris Betts, Allegra Goodman, Robert Olen Butler, Alice Elliott Dark.

Leader Guide, Volume 4 • 0-8066-4578-4
Videocassette, Volume 4 • 0-8066-4579-2

DVD, Volumes 1-2 • 0-8066-4598-9 • Includes Leader Guides for Volumes 1-2
DVD, Volumes 3-4 • 0-8066-4599-7 • Includes Leader Guides for Volumes 3-4

1-800-328-4648   www.augsburgfortress.org

Made in the USA
Lexington, KY
14 July 2010